MOZAMBIQUE
in Pictures

Thomas Streissguth

Twenty-First Century Books

Contents

Twenty-First Century Books
A division of Lerner Publishing Group, Inc.
241 First Avenue North
Minneapolis, MN 55401 U.S.A.

Website address: www.lernerbooks.com

web enhanced @ www.vgsbooks.com

CULTURAL LIFE 46

▶ Family Life. Religion. Language. Literature. Art
and Crafts. Music and Dance. Food. Holidays.
Sports and Recreation.

THE ECONOMY 56

▶ Services. Industry. Agriculture. Transportation
and Communications. Foreign Trade. The Future.

FOR MORE INFORMATION

Library of Congress Cataloging-in-Publication Data

Streissguth, Thomas, 1958-
    Mozambique in pictures / by Tom Streissguth.
        p.   cm. — (Visual geography series)
    Includes bibliographical references and index.
    ISBN 978-1-57505-954-9 (lib. bdg ; alk. paper)
    1. Mozambique—Description and travel. 2. Mozambique—Pictorial works. I. Title.
DT3312.S77 2009
967.9—dc22   2008020393

Manufactured in the United States of America
1 2 3 4 5 6 - BP - 14 13 12 11 10 09

INTRODUCTION

Mozambique, a nation in southeastern Africa, is a land of great variety. Within its borders are tropical beaches and islands, fertile river valleys, broad grasslands, high plains, and rugged mountains. Lions, elephants, and zebras roam the nation's plains. Crocodiles inhabit its many rivers. A vivid tapestry of human culture covers the land.

The culture of Mozambique reflects both African and foreign influences. Farmers had been living in southeastern Africa for more than one thousand years when Portuguese explorers first landed there in the late 1400s. A series of powerful kingdoms had governed the inland forests and river valleys. Since the 700s, the region had traded with distant lands through trading ports on the Indian Ocean.

The Portuguese had little respect for Mozambique's cultural and economic traditions. As colonists settled, farmed, and mined the land, they tried to make Mozambique an outpost of Portugal. They exploited the native people, often forcing them to work on farms or in mines or selling them as slaves. They replaced local chiefs and councils with Portuguese officials. For more than four centuries, these officials made laws and decisions that favored Portugal and its colonists over Mozambique and its native people.

In the early twentieth century, African Mozambicans formed a movement to end Portuguese rule. This movement gathered strength after World War II (1939–1945). An armed uprising erupted in the 1960s. For a decade, Portugal struggled to keep control of Mozambique. But in 1975, Mozambique finally won its independence.

Within a year, nearly all the Portuguese were gone. With their sudden departure, most of Mozambique's skilled human resources—such as engineers, doctors, and business leaders—vanished. (Native Mozambicans had little access to education under Portuguese rule.) As a result, the nation's economy collapsed. Its new government struggled to rebuild and redefine an entire society.

As Mozambique grappled with this challenge, it got caught up in the Cold War (1945–1991). The Cold War was a global power struggle

between two political and economic systems. On one side of this conflict, the Soviet Union promoted Communism, a system in which the government owns all property. On the other side, the United States promoted capitalism, a system of private ownership. The two superpowers were seeking African allies in the 1970s.

Mozambique's newly independent government was Communist. Capitalist nations in Africa and abroad sponsored an armed rebellion against the Mozambican government. This conflict grew into a sixteen-year civil war (1976–1992) that dealt heavy damage and killed nearly one million people.

The war left Mozambique one of the world's poorest nations. Since the 1990s, Mozambique has slowly recovered. A new constitution allows free elections and private property. Nations that were once foes have become important allies, investors, and trading partners. A vibrant national culture has emerged, combining European and African languages and views.

But the country still faces economic and social challenges. Health care is poor, hunger is common, and life expectancy is short. Many Mozambicans live on small farms in isolated areas, vulnerable to extreme weather. Flooding in 2000 and 2001 caused widespread damage to farms and villages in low-lying areas. A severe drought (lack of rain) in 2002 brought famine to parts of southern and eastern Mozambique.

An exploding population complicates such problems. In 2007 Mozambique had a total population of 20.4 million. It was one of the fastest-growing nations in Africa. A high percentage of its citizens are younger than fifteen years. This youthfulness will lead to rapid population growth in the future.

Mozambique also suffers continuing political turmoil. Although the country holds regular elections, the dominant political party faces frequent charges of cheating. Violence has marred several recent elections.

Amid this turmoil, the government is struggling to develop agriculture, industry, and services and to improve basic living conditions. Mozambicans are trying to put their historic troubles behind them and create unity and stability for the future.

THE LAND

Mozambique is a large, Y-shaped nation sprawling along Africa's southeastern coast. Tanzania lies to the north. Malawi nestles in the fork of the Y. Zambia lies to the northwest, Zimbabwe to the west, and South Africa and Swaziland to the southwest. On the east, a long seacoast faces the Mozambique Channel, an arm of the Indian Ocean. Across this channel lies the island nation of Madagascar.

Mozambique covers a land area of 302,739 square miles (784,090 square kilometers), making it slightly larger than the state of Texas. The territory stretches 1,100 miles (1,770 km) from north to south and 680 miles (1,094 km) at its widest from east to west. The coastline is 1,535 miles (2,470 km) long.

◉ Topography

Mozambique is home to a great range of terrain. Between its eastern coast and its western borders, altitudes climb from sea level to 7,992 feet (2,436 meters). The nation covers coastal lowlands, rolling plains,

high plateaus (elevated plains), and steep mountains. All along the coast, a flat and narrow lowland separates the seafront from the rolling savanna (grassland) to the west. This humid coastal strip includes wetlands, palm groves, and dune scrub (shrubs and small trees). Small islands dot the coastal waters, especially those of northern Mozambique.

Inland, the Zambezi River divides the country into three main regions. Northern Mozambique is the right branch of the Y. Central Mozambique is the left branch of the Y, extending to the coast. Southern Mozambique is the stem of the Y.

The East African Plateau stretches across northern Mozambique. In northeastern Mozambique lies a section called the Mavia Plateau. West of this area is a vast tract of miombo woodland, a type of forest that thrives in Africa's dry regions. Several isolated mountains rise above the high plains. Mount Namuli, Mozambique's second-highest peak at 7,936 feet (2,419 m), is one of these.

INDIAN
OCEAN

TANZANIA

AFRICA

EQUATOR

INDIAN
OCEAN

ATLANTIC
OCEAN

MOZAMBIQUE

0 ____ 1000 Miles
0 ____ 1000 KM

CHIZUMULU
ISLAND

LIKOMA
ISLAND

Ruvuma R.

Cape
Delgado
Tunghi Bay

MAVIA
PLATEAU

ZAMBIA

ANGONIA
HIGHLANDS

TETE
HIGHLANDS

Lake Cahora
Bassa

Lake Malawi

NAMULI
HIGHLANDS

Lake
Chilwa

▲ Mount Namuli

IBO ISLAND

Pemba Bay

Fernao
Veloso Bay

Mossuril
Bay

MOZAMBIQUE
ISLAND

Zambezi R.

ZAMBEZI RIVER VALLEY

MALAWI

COASTAL LOWLANDS

Bons Sinais
River

GORONGOSA
MOUNTAINS

Mount ▲
Panga

Pungwe R.

MANICA
PLATEAU

▲ Mount
Binga

CHIMANIMANI
MOUNTAINS

ZIMBABWE

SAVANNA

Pungwe
Bay

Sofala
Bay

Mozambique Channel

BOTSWANA

BAZARUTO
ARCHIPELAGO

BENGUERRA
ISLAND

MADAGASCAR

SOUTHERN PLAINS

Limpopo R.

SOUTH
AFRICA

LEBOMBO
MOUNTAINS

Inhambane
Bay

Cape
Corrientes

Maputo
Bay

Tembe R.

SWAZILAND

Mozambique

Feet	Meters	
9843	3000	Mountains
6562	2000	Uplands
3281	1000	Lowlands
1640	500	

Elevation

N

▲ Mountain peak

0 _____ 200 Miles

0 _____ 200 KM

Cities, towns, and farmland flooded when the Zambezi River topped its banks during a heavy rainy season in 2007. Flooding can ruin farmland, making food scarce for local residents.

Central Mozambique's main feature is the Zambezi River valley, which runs the length of the region. The level terrain and fertile soil of this valley have attracted the country's heaviest settlement. The coastal lowlands extend inland along this valley, meeting the Namuli, Tete, and Angonia highlands near the region's northern and western borders. The heavily forested Angonia Highlands lie along the border of Mozambique and southwestern Malawi. The Tete Highlands rise near the Zambian border. The Gorongosa and Chimanimani mountain ranges emerge south of the Zambezi River valley. The Chimanimani Mountains along the Zimbabwean border include Mount Binga, Mozambique's highest point at 7,992 feet (2,436 m).

Southern Mozambique is the country's flattest region. Here the sluggish Limpopo River runs south through sandy plains and sparsely populated wetlands. The Lebombo Mountains straddle Mozambique's border with South Africa and Swaziland.

Rivers, Bays, and Lakes

The rivers of Mozambique flow west to east, from the highlands to the Indian Ocean. Water levels change dramatically throughout the year. During the rainy season, the rivers swell, often flooding the surrounding countryside. In the dry season, water levels drop and some streams run dry.

Mozambique is home to many rivers, large and small. Among these are two of Africa's major rivers: the Zambezi and the Limpopo.

The Zambezi River flows southeastward through central Mozambique. As it approaches the Indian Ocean, it splits into several branches and forms a wide delta south of the city of Quelimane. Farmers and other settlers have lived in the Zambezi River valley for many centuries. The river serves as a physical barrier and cultural boundary between northern and southern Mozambique. The Cahora Bassa hydroelectric dam lies on the upper Zambezi. It forms a large artificial lake near Mozambique's border with Zambia and Zimbabwe.

Cahora Bassa Dam is Africa's second-largest hydroelectric dam, after Egypt's Aswan High Dam on the Nile River. Likewise, Lake Cahora Bassa is Africa's second-largest artificial lake, after Egypt's Lake Nasser.

The Limpopo River enters Mozambique at its border with Zimbabwe and South Africa. From there it flows southeastward through southern Mozambique. It reaches the coast at the city of Xai-Xai. This wide, slow river swells with runoff during the rainy season. The marshes along its banks make settlement and farming difficult.

Many bays indent the long coast of Mozambique. Tunghi Bay begins just south of Cape Delgado, at the country's northern tip. South of Tunghi Bay lies Pemba Bay, which provides a deepwater anchorage for large ships. The city of Nacala perches on Fernao Veloso Bay, another deep harbor. This bay serves as the main port for landlocked Malawi. The port of Beira overlooks wide Pungwe Bay on the coast of central Mozambique. Southern Mozambique's largest bays are Inhambane Bay and Maputo Bay. The capital city of Maputo and the headland of Cape Corrientes flank Maputo Bay at the southern tip of the country.

The stately city hall *(left)* and a grand Catholic cathedral *(right)* stand guard over downtown Maputo.

Mozambique is home to two large natural lakes. The largest is Lake Malawi, which lies between northern Malawi and northern Mozambique. It contains some of the cleanest freshwater on Earth. The remote lake has no large industries and few towns along its shores, so it's free of most chemicals, fertilizers, and other pollutants that typically cloud large lakes. Lake Chilwa lies south of Lake Malawi, between southern Malawi and northern Mozambique.

Lake Malawi includes two inhabited islands, Likoma and Chizumulu. Mozambican waters surround them. But because missionaries (religious teachers) from Malawi settled on them, the islands remained Malawian territories.

Climate

Mozambican farmers depend heavily on predictable seasonal rainfall patterns. In good years, the rainy season lasts from October to March, and the dry season lasts from April to September. In bad years, the rainy season shortens or disappears. Rivers dry up, and crops suffer. When heavy rains occur, the sunbaked land can't absorb them. This often leads to floods that destroy crops and villages.

In a normal year, Mozambique is drier in the south and along the coast and wetter in the western and northern highlands. Average annual rainfall in southern Mozambique is 24 inches (60 centimeters). The coast receives about 39 inches (100 cm), and the western highlands get

Farmers in south-central Mozambique work in the fields during the rainy season, which typically falls between October and March. Visit www.vgsbooks.com for more information about weather and climate in Mozambique.

55 inches (140 cm). The country's wettest region, the Namuli Highlands in northern Mozambique, averages more than 79 inches (200 cm) per year. Throughout the country, about 80 percent of the rain falls during the rainy season. In the south, the dry season may pass with very little rain—or none at all.

Because Mozambique lies in the Southern Hemisphere (south of the equator), its summer and winter happen at times opposite those of the Northern Hemisphere. Temperatures are warmer during the rainy season (October to March), with readings averaging 81° to 84°F (27° to 29°C). The dry season (April to September) brings cooler temperatures, averaging 64° to 68°F (18° to 20°C). A warm ocean current affects temperatures along the coast, which are higher, on average, than those in the interior.

◑ Flora and Fauna

Mozambique's sprawling territory includes several different kinds of habitat. Coral reefs line the coastal waters. Swampy, sandy lowlands stretch along the shore. River valleys extend inland, crossing grassy savanna and wooded highlands. Unique ecosystems (communities of living things) thrive in each habitat.

The reefs and shallow waters off Mozambique's coast are home to thousands of species of shellfish, such as snails, crabs, and lobsters.

Tropical fish surround a coral reef in the Indian Ocean, off the coast of Mozambique. The reefs attract both sea creatures and tourists.

Palm trees grow in this swampy lowland near the southern town of Tofo, Mozambique.

Dolphins, whales, and sharks are also common here. Dugongs, ocean mammals related to manatees, swim in the waters of the Bazaruto Archipelago, an island group off the southern coast.

Palm trees and mangroves grow along many stretches of the coast. Mangroves are thickets of shrubs and small trees that flourish in salty water. They protect the shore from storm damage and erosion (washing away). Shellfish such as oysters and crabs, as well as shallow-water fish such as mullet, shelter among their sturdy roots.

Mozambique's rivers and marshes teem with amphibians and reptiles, including the huge Nile crocodile, which is dangerous to humans. These freshwater habitats also support some of the country's largest mammals. Hippopotamuses live in river shallows and marshlands. Mozambique's herd of Cape buffalo—nearly wiped out during the civil war—has recovered in the Zambezi River delta.

The nation's savannas are home to elephants, zebras, giraffes, leopards, antelopes, wildebeests (a type of large antelope), lions, and cheetahs. The grasslands also support a wide variety of snakes—some of them dangerous—such as the puff adder and several different kinds of pythons and cobras. Baobab trees flourish in the savannas. These trees are famous for their huge, barrel-shaped trunks.

Mozambique's forests contain large stands of bamboo (a tall, woody type of grass) and other valuable hardwoods, such as ebony,

PROTECTING ANIMALS

Mozambique's large mammals suffered rampant poaching (illegal hunting) during the civil war. Since 1992 many species have recovered, thanks to government efforts to protect them. The nation has created several preserves, which are off-limits to hunters. The largest one, northern Mozambique's Niassa Reserve, is bigger than the state of Massachusetts. It shelters one of the most diverse animal populations in Africa.

The Maputo Elephant Reserve, originally built to protect large herds of freely roaming elephants and rhinoceroses, suffered terribly during the war. The park lies close to the South African border, where some of the worst fighting occurred. Poachers and land mines decimated the animal populations. No rhinos and only about two hundred elephants survived. Thousands of the deadly mines remain buried in the remote areas of this park.

South Africa and Botswana, two of Mozambique's neighbors, are helping the nation restock its national parks and preserves. These nations have shipped thousands of elephants, zebras, and antelopes to the Maputo Elephant Reserve and to Gorongosa National Park.

mahogany, and ironwood. Forest species include the rare Vincent's bush squirrel, which is endemic to Mozambique (lives nowhere else in the world).

More than two hundred native species of plants, orchids, and wildflowers grow in Mozambique. Throughout the country more than five hundred species of and migratory birds survive. Herons, egrets, cranes, and other waterbirds flourish in coastal mangroves. The Namuli apalis is a small, extremely rare bird that lives only on Mount Namuli.

◉ Natural Resources

Mozambique has a great variety of natural resources, many of them untapped. Its most valuable—and most used—resources include fertile land, flowing waters, and deposits of minerals and natural gas.

Mozambique includes large tracts of fertile land. Most of this land lies uncultivated. Many tracts of cropland support subsistence farmers. These are farmers who grow just enough to feed themselves and their families, sometimes with a little surplus to sell. Cultivated farmland also produces cash crops such as tea and sugarcane.

The nation's coastal fishing grounds produce plentiful shellfish. Prawns (large shrimp) are an important export (product sold to other countries). However, Mozambicans have fished their coastal waters heavily for centuries, and many species are dwindling.

Fishers from Benguerra Island prepare their net for a day at sea. Mozambicans sell much of their catch at local markets for export to Asia and Europe.

Mozambique has a wealth of energy resources. But the cost of exploration and mining, plus decades of war and political instability, have prevented the nation from realizing its energy potential. A number of successful natural gas wells operate in southern Mozambique, as do coal mines in the Tete Highlands. Mozambique's many rivers offer potential for hydropower (energy produced by harnessing rushing water), but only the Zambezi River currently generates electricity.

Instability has also prevented Mozambique from developing its wealth of mineral resources. The country has only begun to mine its stores of iron ore, salt, gemstones, gold, phosphate (used in fertilizer), tantalite (useful in making electronics), and bauxite (the basic raw material in aluminum). Near the town of Chibuto, in southern Mozambique's Gaza Province, lies the world's largest deposit of titanium-bearing sands. (Titanium is a light and very strong metal.)

Environmental Issues

Mozambique's long civil war ravaged the country's natural environment. Both sides destroyed habitats and poached animals to sustain their soldiers. The war also drove many people out of their homes and across the borders or to the coastal towns. Refugees overcrowded the cities, strained food and water resources, and cleared large tracts of forest for shelter and fuel. At the same time, a drought turned much of the savanna into desert, hostile to animals and unsuitable for farming.

Since the war, Mozambique has done little to correct its environmental problems. It has created several large game preserves, and it has banned new construction along some of its coastline. But deforestation (clearing trees) continues, and safeguarding forest and water resources takes second place to developing industry. Mozambique's development plans largely overlook environmental protection—even in tourist areas, where healthy habitats attract more visitors.

Tourism promises economic benefits, but it also poses environmental dangers. Building new hotels, resorts, and roads can damage the land and force out farmers. Diving and sport fishing can disrupt ocean ecosystems. Souvenir sales of coral and turtleshell deplete marine life and damage fragile reefs.

In the waters off Mozambique, illegal fishing also takes a toll on the environment. Many unlicensed fishing boats harvest sport, food, and aquarium fish that are protected by law. Oil tankers and cargo ships often damage coral reefs and pollute the water. Pollution from fertilizers, pesticides, sewage, and industrial waste is a growing problem where Mozambique's major rivers meet the sea.

Cities

MAPUTO sits at the mouth of the Tembe River on Maputo Bay in southern Mozambique. As the nation's capital and largest city, Maputo is a province unto itself. Home to 1.1 million people, Maputo includes several different African ethnic groups as well as Portuguese, South Africans, Indians, and Chinese.

Maputo's history began in the late 1700s, when the Portuguese built a fortress there. A town soon grew up around the fort. In 1876 the Portuguese officially named the settlement for explorer Lourenço Marques. In 1898 Lourenço Marques became the capital of Mozambique. After the country won independence from Portugal in 1975, Mozambicans renamed their capital for a legendary African chief, Maputa. The independence struggle and the civil war that followed caused little damage in Maputo, as the city was off-limits to fighting.

Modern Maputo has an international airport and rail links to South Africa. It's home to two major universities and several museums. The city exports a variety of goods, such as hardwoods, sugar, cotton, and coal, through its busy harbor. Factories make cement, shoes, and furniture. In recent years, foreign investment has helped Maputo build new housing to replace some of its slums and outlying shantytowns.

BEIRA (population 436,240), the second-largest city in Mozambique, is also the capital of Sofala Province. This port at the mouth of the Pungwe River serves both central Mozambique and its landlocked neighbors, Zimbabwe, Zambia, and Malawi. A railroad links Beira to Harare, the capital city of Zimbabwe.

After its founding in 1890, Beira quickly became central Mozambique's economic hub. It was home to many Portuguese colonists, and nearby beaches drew tourists from throughout southern Africa. The civil war drove away many of its residents, however. In the 1970s, much of Beira became a ghost town, with unfinished hotels and other commercial buildings housing poor families. Beira slowly rebuilt through the 1990s before floods damaged the city in 2000, leaving thousands of people homeless.

NAMPULA (population 477,900) is the capital of Nampula Province in northern Mozambique. The nation's third-largest city, Nampula serves as a market center for regional farms and as a road and rail hub. Nampula grew from an important junction on a railway linking Mozambique's coast with Malawi. Though Nampula isn't a tourist destination, its National Ethnographic Museum is an important attraction for visitors.

QUELIMANE (population 192,876), a port at the mouth of the Bons Sinais River, is the nation's fourth-largest city. It's also the capital of Zambezia Province in central Mozambique. Quelimane developed on the site of a medieval trading center. A small airport links Quelimane to the rest of the country, and a railroad connects it with northern Mozambique. The city is home to a large fishing fleet as well as a major coconut plantation. Quelimane suffers frequent heavy flooding during the rainy season.

Quelimane is home to the largest grove of coconut palms in the world. Its sandy, salty soil is perfect for coconut trees. These trees can withstand long periods of drought, which is always a danger on the Mozambican coast.

HISTORY AND GOVERNMENT

People have lived on the land that is modern Mozambique for at least ten thousand years. Archaeologists have discovered many remnants of ancient societies, including stone weapons and tools as well as rock paintings. These artifacts offer clues about Mozambique's ancient people. The first group identified in Mozambique by name were the nomadic (wandering) Khoisan people. They were hunter-gatherers who lived in the plains and forests of southern Africa.

◉ Bantu Expansion

By the 1500s B.C., Bantu-speaking peoples from the Niger River delta in western Africa were moving east and south through the continent. Around the A.D. 300s, they reached the Zambezi River valley and the Indian Ocean. As the Bantu-speaking migrants settled the valley, the Khoisan people moved to more remote regions. The Khoisan eventually left Mozambique and other Bantu-dominated areas entirely, retreating to the Kalahari Desert and other isolated parts of southern Africa.

The expansion of the Bantu speakers brought both technological and social changes to southern Africa. The group knew how to make iron tools and weapons. They established farms and permanent villages. Bantu-speaking peoples organized their societies around lineages. (A lineage is a group of people who trace their history to a single ancestor.) The strongest lineages formed clans (groups of allied families). These clans ruled their members through chiefs and councils.

The Bantu speakers spread their knowledge and customs throughout the region. Eventually, distinct ethnic groups emerged, including the Makonde and Yao of the north, the Macua-Lomue of northern and central Mozambique, and the Chopi, Tsonga, and Tonga of the south.

Arab Sultanates

After the expansion of the Bantu speakers, traders from the Arabian Peninsula were exploring the Mozambican coast. The Arabs had already formed a large trading network around the Indian Ocean.

QVILOA

Kilwa Kisiwani (in Tanzania) was the richest city in eastern Africa from A.D. 1000 to 1500. Goods from Sofala and other ports were sent there. This bird's-eye view of the city was published in a 1572 atlas known as the *Civitates Orbis Terrarum* (Cities of the World) in Cologne, Germany.

Beginning in the 700s, they added outposts at Ibo Island, Mozambique Island, and Sancul and Sangage islands, and the mainland towns of Quelimane, Angoche, and Sofala. These trading posts linked southern Africa with the cities of Arabia, Persia (modern Iran), and India.

The Arabs exchanged their cloth, glass, ceramics, and weapons for African gold, rhinoceros horn, ivory (elephant tusks), palm oil, and slaves. The Arabs made treaties (agreements) with African chiefs. The treaties exchanged goods and weapons for the right to trade in the chiefs' territories. Key trading routes developed on the Zambezi River and between Sofala and eastern Zimbabwe.

Sofala became a key storage and transfer point. From warehouses in this port, the Arab merchants shipped their goods northward to Kilwa (in modern Tanzania). Kilwa was the collection point for all East African goods bound for Asian markets. The trade made Sofala a wealthy and influential city.

Arab sultans (kings) ruled Sofala and the other major trading ports. The Arabs practiced Islam, a religion founded by the Arab prophet Muhammad in the 600s. They converted some of the local populations to this faith. Other Africans held to animism. (Animism is a worldview in which spirits inhabit natural places, beings, things, and the everyday world.) The Swahili language developed from contact between Arabs and East Africans.

After the Arabs arrived, a Bantu-speaking ethnic group called the Maravi rose to power in northern Mozambique. The Maravi originally ruled the region around Lake Malawi. Eventually their strong kings and unified society overcame the fragmented Macua-Lomue society. The Maravi, cooperating with Arab merchants on the coast, controlled the ivory trade in northern Mozambique. They shipped ivory downriver on rafts or overland, using human bearers or pack animals.

◉ Shona Dynasties

The Shona people arose from an alliance of several Bantu-speaking clans. Shona authority emerged in the 800s in Zimbabwe and southern Mozambique. The various Shona groups united under the kings of the Karanga clan. By the 900s, the Karanga dynasty (family of rulers) controlled a vast territory and its trade in gold and ivory.

The Karanga kings were military, political, and religious leaders. They collected gold and cattle as tribute (a kind of tax) from the many peoples they conquered. They built a capital at Great Zimbabwe, a vast walled stronghold near the center of modern Zimbabwe. But the population of the region surrounding Great Zimbabwe grew so quickly that it exhausted the soil and other natural resources.

The Shona people abandoned Great Zimbabwe in the 1300s. At this time, the Mbire clan began to lead the alliance. A Mbire king named Nyatsimba Mutota conquered new territory along the upper Zambezi River in the early 1400s. This act earned him the title Munhumutapa, which means "conquerer." The Shona kingdom gave way to the Munhumutapa Empire.

Thousands of people lived in the city of **Great Zimbabwe** between the 1000s and the 1400s. It was the hub for the Shona, who ruled Zimbabwe and Mozambique at that time.

Nyatsimba Mutota's son, Matope Nyanyenwe, extended the empire to include all of central Mozambique in the mid-1400s. He set up members of the Mbire clan as tribute-paying local chiefs. These chiefs controlled trade with the coast and collected taxes on goods moving through their local marketplaces.

Munhumutapa agents also oversaw foreign trade. The empire grew even more rich and powerful by controlling trade in Mozambique—especially the exchange of African ivory and gold for Arabian salt, pottery, and other goods. The port of Sofala remained a very important link in the Indian Ocean trade network.

In the late 1400s, the Changamire dynasty arose at Great Zimbabwe and began to challenge the Munhumutapa Empire. Changa, the founder of this dynasty, captured and killed his rival, the Munhumutapa king Mukombero. Changa himself later died in battle.

A war between the Munhumutapa and the Changamire dynasties continued for many years. This conflict allowed the smaller realms to break free of the empire. It also weakened these dynasties' defenses against foreign invasion.

◉ The Portuguese Conquest

In 1498 the Portuguese explorer Vasco da Gama became the first European to sail around the Cape of Good Hope (the southern tip of Africa). He then sailed northward along Africa's Indian Ocean coast. In 1500 another Portuguese navigator, Pedro Álvares Cabral, set out to follow da Gama's route to the East Indies (southern and southeastern Asia). In the southern Atlantic Ocean, storms and currents carried Cabral off course. He eventually landed in Brazil, where he founded a Portuguese colony.

Cabral then returned to Portugal, while several of his ships rounded the Cape of Good Hope and landed at Sofala. There the Portuguese discovered a busy gold market between the coast and the interior of Africa. Their report of this discovery to the king of Portugal inspired a rush to settle the region.

The Portuguese returned with many well-armed caravels (sailing ships). They scattered the smaller,

VASCO DA GAMA

When Portuguese explorer Vasco da Gama landed on Mozambique Island, he posed as a Muslim. But his gifts of a simple tin bell, a woolen hood, and copper bracelet made the sultan of Mozambique Island suspicious. The local people soon grew unhappy with da Gama and his crew, who had little of value to trade in the marketplace. Fearing for their lives, the men sailed away, firing a few cannon shots at the town in revenge.

weaker Arabian ships and claimed a piece of the busy Indian Ocean trading network. In 1505 Francisco de Almeida arrived to conquer the East African coast. The Portuguese drove away the Arab sultans who ruled Sofala and other port cities. Portuguese ships traveling to the East Indies began stopping at these ports to repair their ships and restock their supplies.

The Portuguese soon expanded their presence in southeastern Africa. In 1507 they built a fortress and founded a town on a small coral island at the mouth of Mossuril Bay. The island was known as Mozambique Island. The Portuguese named their settlement Saint Sebastian of Mozambique. Jesuit missionaries arrived and brought with them their Roman Catholic faith.

The Portuguese also took over the Arabs' role in the gold and ivory trade. Portuguese merchants collected gold and ivory in large warehouses in Sofala. Then they shipped the goods to India, where the Portuguese traded them for spices—at that time, the most valuable product of all.

HISTORY OF A NAME

Musa Alibiki, an Arab sultan, is the namesake of Mozambique Island. The Portuguese built their first settlement on that island and named the settlement after it. They called their string of southeast African settlements Portuguese East Africa. In 1951, when Portugal declared this entire collection of colonies a province of Portugal, it named the province Mozambique.

Francisco de Almeida helped bring the East African coast under Portuguese control in the early 1500s. By establishing forts and trading posts there, the Portuguese became strong players in the Indian spice trade.

Throughout the 1500s, Europeans explored the African interior from the coastal towns of Portuguese East Africa. Gold prospectors, ivory merchants, and slave traders arrived from Europe. But Portugal made more money trading spices in the East Indies, so it did little to develop its African ports directly.

Instead, the king of Portugal let individuals settle and do business in Portuguese East Africa. The settlers promised to pay one-fifth of their income to Portugal's treasury. Eager for fertile land, colonists built *fazendas* (plantations, or large commercial farms) in the interior. They enslaved Africans to work these plantations. The fazendas operated independently of the colonial government.

In 1561 Portgual began sending small bands of soldiers inland to protect the gold routes. In the 1570s, Portugal set out to subdue the Shona people's Munhumutapa Empire. Francisco Barreto led a campaign that forced the Munhumutapa chiefs to give up some control of the gold trade. As the Arabs had done earlier, the Portuguese offered military aid in exchange for trading rights. Portuguese soldiers helped the Shona defeat rebellious chiefs and conquer new territories.

Francisco Barreto *(on the white horse)* **and his Portuguese troops fought African soldiers in the 1570s. The king of Portugal had sent Barreto to search for African gold mines, but Barreto died in 1573 before locating them.**

In 1580 Portugal and Spain united when the king of Spain, who also had royal Portuguese blood, assumed the throne of Portugal. Portugal and Spain remained independent nations, but their fortunes grew closely intertwined. With much more profitable colonies in South America and the East Indies, the king paid little attention to his holdings in Africa.

Portugal itself entered a period of economic decline. Its African ports fell into disuse. Settlers and merchants began to abandon the colony. Meanwhile, Dutch merchant ships challenged Portuguese control of the Indian Ocean. In 1604 the Dutch began a series of attacks against the Saint Sebastian fortress on Mozambique Island. Though they failed to capture the fort, they kept harassing it and other Portuguese ports. Soon the British joined in, eager to expand their empire in Africa.

In the early 1600s, a new slave market developed in Portuguese East Africa. Raiders supplying traders on the coast kidnapped healthy men, women, and children from the interior. Sometimes entire villages disappeared. Many Africans captured via raids or as prisoners of war traveled through the colony's ports to Brazilian plantations. Arabian and Turkish buyers brought other slaves to the Middle East.

Fighting for the Colony

In 1629 the king of the Munhumutapa Empire surrendered his territory to the Portuguese. The king of Portugal began leasing *prazos* (vast land estates) to *prazeiros*. These landlords arrived from Portugal and from other Portuguese colonies. They established farms and mines and forced the Africans living on their estates to work for them.

In 1640 Portugal separated from Spain. Portuguese East Africa, for its part, remained isolated from Portugal. Portugal had little money to invest in the colony. Malaria and other tropical diseases took a heavy toll on colonists. And the prazeiros were paying little heed to Portuguese authority. They disregarded both the king and the colony's local ruler, the governor-general.

The prazeiros became chiefs of small kingdoms. Prazeiros ran private armies, courts of justice, and markets. They fought alongside African chiefs with whom they allied. Many prazeiros took African names and titles, participated in traditional African religious rites, and intermarried with African clans.

By 1700 Portugal fully governed only Mozambique Island. (Though Portugal claimed a far larger territory, it had little real control over most of Portuguese East Africa.) Brazil had become a more important source of gold. Few settlers came to Portuguese East Africa in hopes of becoming wealthy farmers or landlords. The Dutch, who had seized the East Indies spice trade, built a post at Delagoa Bay

MOZAMBICAN SLAVE TRADE

The slave trade flourished in Mozambique in the early 1800s. At the peak of the trade, raiders took more than twenty-five thousand people per year from their inland villages to the coast. In the port towns, slave traders sold their captives to merchant ships. Then the human cargo made a grueling voyage around the Cape of Good Hope and across the Atlantic Ocean to plantations in the Caribbean islands and in Brazil. Portugal outlawed the Mozambican slave trade in 1842, but it continued secretly for decades.

(modern Maputo Bay). British merchants also traded there.

In the meantime, the Changamire dynasty grew powerful and began to challenge Portuguese control of trade in the interior. Caravaners brought gold, ivory, rhino horn, and slaves to the ports in exchange for weapons, cloth, and luxury items in demand at the Changamire royal court.

Though settlement had slowed to a trickle, some Europeans still hoped to profit from southeastern Africa. In the late 1700s, settlers founded a town named after the sixteenth-century Portuguese explorer Lourenço Marques on the northern edge of Delagoa Bay. In 1777 a fleet of Austrian ships attacked the town and drove out the Portuguese. An Austrian trading company set up a headquarters there. The headquarters closed several years later, and the Portuguese returned to Lourenço Marques.

In 1833 Lourenço Marques suffered another assault—this time by the Zulu Kingdom to the south (in modern South Africa). Under the mighty leader Soshangane, Zulu forces overcame the Portuguese city's defenses. In the countryside, the Zulus raided farms, stole livestock, and enslaved their prisoners of war. The Zulu raids further weakened Portuguese influence in the south. But Zulu forces were also fighting the British. This invited further British interference and competition.

Widespread conflict over European colonies in Africa led to an important conference in Germany's capital, Berlin, from 1884 to 1885. The Berlin Conference confirmed Portugal's right to govern Portuguese East Africa.

Labor Unrest

In the late nineteenth century, Portugal was still unable to develop and govern its East African colony. The Portuguese rented the colony's resources to private companies. In many places, these businesses served as the government.

An 1892 British newspaper published this engraving of African slaves arriving for work at a Portuguese fort in Mozambique.

In the 1880s and 1890s, Portugal granted huge prazos to the Niassa Company, the Zambezi Company, and the Mozambique Company. These prazos covered the northern two-thirds of modern Mozambique. The companies' charters gave them the right to exploit all the resources—natural and human—within their territories. In return, Portugal demanded a share of the companies' profits. It also required the companies to settle Portuguese families and provide public education and administration.

The colony's laws allowed the Portuguese to forcibly enlist African workers. The companies rounded up locals to work in mines and on plantations. They seized and sold the harvests of small family farms. They also imposed a hut tax on each household. This tax made wage labor necessary for families who had no cash because their wealth lay in livestock or other assets.

The bleak labor conditions in Portuguese East Africa drove many workers across the border into Rhodesia (modern Zimbabwe) and South Africa. Mines and plantations in these neighboring lands needed laborers and welcomed the migrants. This migration continued for several decades. It separated and displaced many families. Parts of the central and northern regions returned to wilderness as their African residents fled.

Meanwhile, the southern region was growing more important to Portuguese East Africa. The Portuguese moved their colonial capital from Mozambique Island to Lourenço Marques in 1898.

◎ World Wars and Anticolonialism

In the early twentieth century, conflict was brewing in Europe. World War I (1914–1918) broke out in 1914 as events led Germany to declare war on France. Most of the other European nations quickly took sides. France and Britain led the Allies, which opposed Germany and the Central powers. Portugal joined the Allies and drafted thousands of African men to fight. This forced recruitment sparked violent resistance.

António Salazar

World War I ended with an Allied victory. But the postwar period brought political turmoil to Portugal. This turmoil resulted in a military dictatorship under António Salazar. An army officer who had also served as finance minister, Salazar was determined to make Portuguese East Africa more productive.

Portugal began to settle many farmers in the south and the Zambezi River valley. Portugal also extended citizenship to African residents who agreed to learn Portuguese, surrender African religion, and accept salaried jobs. The colonial justice system treated these *assimilados* differently than it treated *indigenas*, who kept their traditional African ways.

In 1939 World War II erupted in Europe. Once again, Germany and its allies (the Axis powers) fought a group of Allies, which included France and Britain. Instead of joining the Allies, Portugal stayed neutral. Six years later, the war ended with another Allied victory.

The end of the war brought many demands for independence by Europe's African colonies. Several colonies became self-ruling states. But Portugal, still led by Salazar, refused to grant independence to Portuguese East Africa. Instead, in 1951 Salazar declared the colony a province of Portugal. Portugal named the new province Mozambique. Poverty and unemployment in postwar Portugal prompted many Portuguese to move to Mozambique.

The Portuguese made money fairly easily in Mozambique. They ran productive farms, plantations, and mines there. These businesses still used forced labor. The provincial government also profited from the work of Mozambicans in South African gold mines. Mozambique charged taxes and fees for the laborers it sent to South Africa. South Africa paid with a share of the gold it shipped through Mozambican ports. These payments became a vital source of income for Mozambique.

In the meantime, the miners faced difficult and dangerous working conditions. Cave-ins, fires, and equipment breakdowns plagued South

Africa's gold mines. The miners—and other Mozambican migrants laboring as farmhands and factory workers—also faced hostility from South Africans. Many South Africans saw the migrants as competitors for jobs.

In the 1950s, poor working conditions, poverty, and injustice inspired Mozambicans to form several groups demanding independence. Most of these groups operated in neighboring countries. Their members feared arrest and imprisonment by a secret police force that upheld Portuguese rule in Mozambique.

The FRELIMO Revolt

In 1962 three independence groups merged to form the Front for the Liberation of Mozambique (better known by its Portuguese acronym, FRELIMO). FRELIMO was based in Dar es Salaam, the capital of Tanzania. Its leader was Eduardo Mondlane. The group took up arms in September 1964, after a skirmish with Portuguese forces in the northern Mozambican village of Chai. Throughout the 1960s, FRELIMO attracted thousands of new members. The group established several zones of control in northern and central Mozambique.

Portugal responded with a military counterattack. The provincial government forcibly resettled thousands of families away from the rebel-controlled zones. This action was meant to deny FRELIMO support and recruits. Portugal also encouraged dissent and rivalry among the FRELIMO leaders. It sent assassins and undercover agents outside Mozambique to disrupt the opposition. In 1969 Portuguese agents killed Mondlane with a letter bomb.

Under a new leader, Samora Machel, FRELIMO increased its sabotage (acts meant to hamper the Portuguese war effort). The group also launched raids on public works, including the Cahora Bassa Dam. Portugal strengthened its military posts and recruited new troops. Many of these new recruits came from neighboring nations that opposed Mozambican independence. But Portuguese forces were spread too thinly over Mozambique's huge territory. FRELIMO steadily gained ground and access to resources.

Samora Machel

The cost of the war—in lives and money— raised protests in Portugal. In 1974 Salazar's opponents overthrew him. The new Portuguese government agreed to grant Mozambique self-rule. Portugal also agreed to recognize FRELIMO as the sole governing party, despite other independence groups' demands for representation.

FRELIMO independence fighters captured two Portuguese soldiers *(center, without guns)* during Mozambique's war for independence.

On June 25, 1975, Mozambique officially became an independent country. FRELIMO established a one-party government under President Samora Machel. In 1976 Mozambicans changed the name of their capital from Lourenço Marques to Maputo.

During that first year of independence, most of Mozambique's Portuguese residents fled. They took with them their money, their skills, and their administrative experience, leaving Mozambique in dire need of investment and a skilled workforce. The nation's economy collapsed. The new government struggled to rebuild its administration and reorganize its society.

Machel sought international allies to help his country meet its many challenges. At the same time, both Communist and capitalist nations around the world were seeking allies in Africa. FRELIMO was Communist, and Machel allied Mozambique with the Communist Soviet Union.

Communism is a political and economic theory whose goal is to create equality among people. Communists believe that community ownership of all property supports that goal. The FRELIMO government nationalized Mozambique's industries, taking them out of private hands and putting them under government control. It seized private farms, created state-run cooperative farms, and forced farmers to move from their homes to these cooperatives.

Mozambique ended the tribal councils and chiefdoms that had traditionally governed local areas. Members of the FRELIMO party formed committees to govern each province and town. And because Communism opposes religion, FRELIMO closed down Catholic churches and schools and ended all missionary activity.

Civil War

Two of Mozambique's neighbors, Rhodesia (modern Zimbabwe) and South Africa, were not pleased with the new Mozambican government. These neighbors saw the FRELIMO regime as both a political and an economic threat.

Both Rhodesia and South Africa were governed by white minority parties that oppressed their black African citizens. These nations opposed African movements for independence and democratic representation, including those mounted by their own citizens. Mozambique provided a safe haven for Rhodesian and South African rebels. This prompted Rhodesia and South Africa to form militias, which staged hit-and-run attacks along the Mozambican border.

Mozambique also supported a United Nations–sponsored ban on trade with Rhodesia. It denied landlocked Rhodesia use of Mozambican ports on the Indian Ocean.

Seeking to stop the growth of groups opposed to its government, Rhodesia founded the Mozambican National Resistance (better known by its Portuguese acronym, RENAMO). This organization recruited many of the militia forces operating along the border. Rhodesia and South Africa also began an economic boycott against (refused to do any business with) Mozambique. The boycott starved Mozambique of much-needed trade and investment.

Its opposition to FRELIMO earned RENAMO some support from Mozambicans. Many rural peasants supported RENAMO by force or out of fear. Others saw the group as a way to end FRELIMO's unpopular Communist policies. Some RENAMO supporters were members of Mozambican independence parties. These parties had been left out of Mozambique's new government and made illegal.

RENAMO units staged raids on harbors, bridges, power plants, and other public works. RENAMO and FRELIMO units clashed in the countryside. From time to time, both sides took control of towns and used them as recruiting centers.

As the conflict dragged on into the 1980s, Mozambique split into RENAMO- and FRELIMO-controlled areas. RENAMO grew quite powerful in the countryside. Mozambique's economy declined as the war took a heavy toll of life and property. Many Mozambicans left the country. More than one million refugees fled across the borders

This 1989 photo shows **Mozambican refugees at a camp in Malawi.** Hundreds of thousands of Mozambicans fled their homes to avoid being caught up in the violence of the civil war.

to Tanzania, Malawi, Zambia, Rhodesia (renamed Zimbabwe when it gained independence in 1980), and South Africa.

In the meantime, Mozambicans who stayed put were growing frustrated with the FRELIMO government. Its Communist policies shredded Mozambique's social fabric and did nothing to revive the economy. To head off a revolt, President Machel lifted the ban on religion and reinstated village chiefs and councils. The government also allowed people to own and farm private plots of land.

In 1984, hoping to end South Africa's support for RENAMO, Machel signed the Nkomati Accord with South Africa's prime minister, P. W. Botha. Both sides promised to stop interfering in each other's political conflicts. The treaty did not stop the fighting, however. South African supplies and troops continued to bolster RENAMO. The group strengthened its hold on the countryside and began threatening the capital, Maputo.

On October 19, 1986, a plane crash in the Lebombo Mountains killed Machel and several Mozambican government ministers. Some FRELIMO members believed the South African government, still an opponent of FRELIMO, led the plane astray with a false radio beacon. The event aggravated tensions between the two countries.

Joaquim Chissano succeeded Machel as president of Mozambique. The FRELIMO government used the change in leadership as a way to open negotiations with RENAMO. Other factors bolstered this dialogue. In the late 1980s, the Soviet Union, FRELIMO's key Communist ally, was collapsing. So was Mozambique's own Communist experiment. Mozambicans were refusing to join cooperative farms, surrender their religious practices, or abandon their traditional chiefs.

In 1990 the government decided to change Mozambique's political and economic system. It wrote a new constitution legalizing opposition parties, reinstating private property, and setting up elections. The country also allowed private businesses. In October 1992, FRELIMO and RENAMO signed a peace treaty in Rome, Italy, officially ending the civil war.

Difficulty in Peacetime

Mozambican refugees gradually returned home during the 1990s. Many nations offered financial aid and trade pacts to help Mozambique's struggling economy. RENAMO established a political party led by Afonso Dhlakama. It began running candidates in national elections in 1994.

Chissano won the 1994 presidential election. FRELIMO won a majority (more than half) of the legislative seats in the national assembly, called the Assembly of the Republic. Many RENAMO leaders accused FRELIMO of cheating during the election. The country managed to avoid widespread violence despite this political conflict.

Joaquim Chissano

In 1998 the legislature rewrote Mozambique's election law. A voter registration drive resulted in a high turnout in the 1999 election. Voters elected Chissano to a second five-year term as president.

Mozambicans lined up to vote in the 1999 presidential elections. The country's largest turnout of voters reelected Joaquim Chissano of FRELIMO.

Thousands of people displaced by floods in 2000 line up for food in this temporary refugee camp. Weather-related events, such as floods and droughts, hamper Mozambique's efforts to recover from colonial exploitation, civil war, and governmental disputes.

The RENAMO party filed a complaint with the Supreme Court, which upheld the election results.

Climate posed Mozambique's most difficult challenges in the early twenty-first century. Frequent storms and flooding in the southern and central regions displaced thousands of people in 2000 and 2001. Drought conditions that started in 2002 and continued for several years brought many families to the brink of starvation. International aid organizations shipped food, medicine, and other important supplies to the affected areas. They also helped many farmers plant new crops and rebuild their homes.

In Mozambique's 2004 election, FRELIMO candidate Armando Guebuza won the presidency. FRELIMO also won a majority in the Mozambique legislature. The country's economy finally began to grow. Overland trade with southern Africa, as well as overseas trade via the Indian Ocean, brought in much-needed foreign money. Tourism grew into a successful industry, especially along the seacoast. In 2008 flooding in the Zambezi River valley displaced more than fifty thousand Mozambicans. Despite these and other natural, political, and economic challenges, modern Mozambique remains a modest success story among Africa's many former European colonies.

For links to articles containing up-to-date information about Mozambique's political affairs, visit www.vgsbooks.com.

Government

Mozambicans govern their country by the constitution of 1990. This document established a multiparty system with executive, legislative, and judicial branches. The president is the head of state (chief public representative) and head of government (chief decision-making authority). Citizens elect the president to a five-year term by popular vote.

The president leads the country in cooperation with a prime minister, whom the president appoints. Ministers represent the various government departments. The president appoints these ministers as well as governors of the country's eleven provinces. All adults at least eighteen years of age have the right to vote.

The Assembly of the Republic is Mozambique's legislature. Its 250 members serve five-year terms. Mozambique follows a system of proportional representation. The number of votes collected by each party in a national election determines the number of seats the party wins. Mozambique also has thirty-three municipal assemblies, which pass laws for cities and provinces.

The Supreme Court is Mozambique's highest court. It hears cases dealing with constitutional questions or international law issues. The judicial system includes courts on the provincial, district, and municipal levels.

Mozambicans divide their land into eleven provinces, one of which is the capital city of Maputo. The provinces are further divided into 129 districts, 405 administrative posts, and many hundreds of localities. The territory also includes thirty-three municipalities (larger towns and cities).

THE PEOPLE

Mozambique has a population of about 20.4 million, which is growing 2.1 percent every year. Researchers expect the population to reach 27.5 million by the year 2025. This is a high growth rate among African countries. Like many other nations on the continent, Mozambique has a young population. About 43 percent of Mozambicans are younger than fifteen years old.

The country's population density is 67 people per square mile (26 people per sq. km). Mozambique is much less crowded than neighboring Tanzania, Malawi, and Zambia. The population is spread fairly evenly over the country, with somewhat higher densities in the north and along the seacoast. Zambezia Province and Nampula Province on the northern coast are home to nearly half the population. Tete Province in north central Mozambique and Niassa Province next to Lake Malawi have the nation's lowest population densities.

Though Mozambique's population has always been more rural than urban, that status is steadily changing. In 1975, when Mozambique became independent, 91 percent of Mozambicans lived in rural areas, while 9 percent lived in cities. Thirty years later, only 65 percent of Mozambicans lived in rural areas, while 35 percent lived in cities. The civil war drove many people out of the country as refugees. As the economy improves and peace endures, many of these refugees are returning, swelling the cities and straining local resources and basic services.

⬤ Social Divisions

The basic social divides in Mozambique are not ethnic ones. Rather, they're geographic. Mozambicans generally identify themselves as northerners or southerners. The Zambezi River marks the boundary between north and south. Mozambicans further identify themselves as country people or city people.

Country life and city life in Mozambique differ sharply in some ways but share some traits too. In the countryside, most families live

Residents of this **village on Mozambique Island live in traditional homes** made with local materials.

in small homes in isolated villages. They have limited access to basic services such as electricity, running water, and public transportation. Jobs are scarce, so many young people move to cities when they become adults.

Cities offer more opportunity, but many newcomers from the countryside wind up in urban shantytowns. Shantytowns are settlements of poor people, usually on the outskirts of cities. Their homes are made of scrap material, and they often lack electricity, telephones, running water, or proper sanitation (waste removal). Shantytowns tend to be overcrowded and suffer from high rates of crime and disease.

Mozambicans identify themselves not only geographically but also ethnically. The many ethnic groups in Mozambique result from centuries of African migrations into different parts of the country. Contact with Arabs and settlement by Europeans complicated the ethnic patchwork.

In the twenty-first century, more than a dozen distinct communities survive. About 99 percent of Mozambicans are members of African ethnic groups. The remaining 1 percent are of Portuguese ancestry. Mozambicans call people with both African and European ancestry *mestiços*.

Above: **A run-down apartment building in Beira** provides housing for some city residents. *Below:* The Makonde people are matrilineal, which means they trace their ancestry through their mothers. **This Makonde woman** has traditional facial tattoos and a pierced lip. Both are considered symbols of beauty and fierceness.

The Macua descend from a Bantu-speaking group that emerged in central Mozambique. It is the largest group in the north. Because the Macua live far from the capital, they have long struggled to achieve a strong voice in Mozambique's government. The Yao and Makonde groups live along the Ruvuma River at the Tanzanian border. The Yao played an important historical role in trade between the coast and the interior. Many elements of their modern culture, including Islam, came from their contact with Arab merchants. These northern groups are matrilineal. They pass down property and wealth to daughters before sons.

The Shona are the largest ethnic group in the central Mozambican provinces of Sofala and Manica. The Sena and Ndau groups live mainly in the Zambezi River valley. In this valley, Portuguese settlers built vast farming estates and worked them with African laborers. As a result, the Sena and Ndau absorbed many everyday customs from the Portuguese. The Europeans in turn adopted some religious traditions from the Africans and also spoke their languages. Some ethnic groups, such as the Chikunda and Nungue, actually formed in the communities of slave laborers.

The Tsonga are the largest ethnic group in the south. They're also one of Mozambique's largest groups overall. The Tsonga people live in South Africa and Zimbabwe too. Members of this group have a long history of crossing borders as guest laborers. The Tsonga divide themselves further into Shangan, Rjonga, Hlengwe, and Tsua according to the languages they speak. The Rjonga group is the largest in Maputo and the city's surrounding region. Other ethnic groups in southern Mozambique are the Chopi and the Tonga. Both groups raise cattle and farm small plots of land, growing enough to support their families and selling any surplus in public markets.

Mozambique's small population of Portuguese people are descendants of the settlers and farmers who began arriving in the 1500s. In 1975 about 250,000 Portuguese lived in Mozambique. More than 90 percent of these people fled during the civil war that followed Mozambique's independence.

Since the war's end in 1992, many Portuguese, British, Americans, Germans, and South Africans have settled in Maputo and other cities to start new businesses. The ports are also home to small numbers of Arab, Indian, Pakistani, and Chinese merchants and traders.

◉ Health

Mozambique's decades of war have led to many ongoing public health problems. The country has never had many hospitals, even in large cities. In rural areas, many clinics shut down as doctors fled and soldiers looted medical equipment.

Since 1992 the country has struggled to rebuild its health-care and sanitation systems. But Mozambique still has a shortage of doctors and trained health workers. And a chronic lack of clean water has caused regular outbreaks of cholera (a deadly diarrheal infection) and other waterborne sicknesses.

Visit www.vgsbooks.com to find links to statistical information about the population in Mozambique.

Patients at a malaria clinic sponsored by international groups await treatment. In Mozambique many children suffer from the deadly disease, which is spread by mosquitoes.

Mozambique is struggling to control other diseases too. Malaria is a growing concern. The mosquito-borne parasite (orgamism living off another organism) that causes this disease is developing resistance to the medicines used to treat it.

Acquired immunodeficiency syndrome (AIDS), a disease caused by the human immunodeficiency virus (HIV), is a serious problem in Mozambique. More than 16 percent of Mozambicans between the ages of fifteen and forty-nine years carry HIV. This is one of the highest HIV rates in the world. To hinder the spread of the virus through sexual contact, Mozambique has started a public education program. The program promotes abstinence (avoiding sex) by the young, condom use, and faithfulness in marriage. Still the rate of infection continues to rise.

Very few Mozambican women get adequate health care during pregnancy and childbirth. As a result, about ten women per one thousand die in childbirth, and 108 babies per

DANGER: LAND MINES

Many years after the end of Mozambique's civil war, land mines still pose great danger for rural residents. During the war, both FRELIMO and RENAMO laid millions of mines under roads and trails used by their enemies. The mines were intended not only to injure and kill opponents but to make it impossible for farmers to work their fields. Flooding in the early twenty-first century displaced many of these mines, making them even harder to find and disarm. Every month about twenty people step on land mines. More than half of these people die from their injuries.

A women's group talks with villagers about the importance of a healthy diet. Malnutrition has led to higher death rates in rural areas of the country.

one thousand die before their first birthday. These are very high rates compared to most other countries. Children who survive infancy face a constant threat of malnutrition. Many Mozambican farmers can grow barely enough food to sustain their families. Natural disasters such as floods and cyclones, as well as artificial hazards such as land mines, make it even harder for rural families to survive and thrive. Mozambique's overall life expectancy is about forty-two years for men and forty-four years for women. These figures are among the lowest in the world.

The government of Mozambique is spending heavily to improve public health. About 18 percent of the national budget goes to training doctors and improving medical facilities. Mozambique also benefits from international aid programs designed to improve public health care in isolated and poor areas. These programs are building clean water wells, vaccinating people against diseases, and building new clinics.

Education

Under Portuguese rule, Mozambique had no public school system. Jesuit missionaries built some small private schools. These mission schools were the only way for most people to learn basic skills through the mid-1900s. Illiteracy was high, and 90 percent of Mozambicans couldn't read or write in any language.

After Mozambique won independence in 1975, its government began building a public education system and requiring children to attend primary school. The result was a steady rise in the literacy rate. In 2005 about 50 percent of Mozambicans could read and write.

Mozambique has struggled to build enough schools and train enough teachers to serve its growing population of school-age youth. About 61 percent of all primary-age children attend school. The early grades teach basic writing, reading, and math skills.

The law requires all children to take exams after completing the seventh grade. The exams allow them to go on to secondary school, which lasts for three years. Secondary school subjects include history, science, math, Portuguese, English, and geography.

Secondary school students take another round of exams after completing the tenth grade. Qualified students may then continue to pre-university school, which lasts two years. The pre-university level teaches history, basic science, and languages, including Portuguese and English. These courses prepare students for university studies—if they can find a place. Mozambique's ten universities don't have enough room to accept all the qualified students. As a result, many young adults go abroad for university studies. Others enter technical training institutes.

At these institutes, each student trains for a specific profession and earns a certificate qualifying him or her to work in that field.

THE WAR AND SCHOOLS

The civil war took a heavy toll on Mozambique's fledgling public education system. Combat and sabotage destroyed many schools and killed or drove away many teachers. Mozambique is working hard to rebuild. In 2007 it raised 677 new primary schools and forty-five new secondary schools. For the first time in Mozambique's history, a majority of its primary-age children attend school. However, Mozambique still has a shortage of classroom space and qualified teachers. Also, many families send only sons to school. They keep their daughters at home to care for crops and livestock.

Boys at this school in western Mozambique work together in the classroom. Education is hard to come by for many children. Schools, materials, and qualified teachers are scarce.

CULTURAL LIFE

Mozambique's unique culture reflects influences from both Africa and overseas. Many centuries of African migrations, trading with Arabs, and colonization by the Portuguese created a vivid cultural tapestry in Mozambique.

The nation's struggle for independence and its civil war brought almost thirty years of strife. The prolonged violence affected nearly every aspect of cultural life. But Mozambique's distinctive lifeways survived the physical, political, and social upheaval. In modern Mozambique, old and new cultural practices thrive side by side.

Family Life

The basic social unit in Mozambique is the extended family. It includes the immediate family plus grandparents, uncles, aunts, and cousins. The family owns property in common. A group of families who descend from a single important ancestor is called a lineage. A group of related lineages is called a clan. Young people marry outside their clans, usually

to spouses selected by their elders. Northern Mozambican families are generally matrilineal. Southern families are generally patrilineal. They trace their ancestry through their fathers, and they pass down property and wealth to sons before daughters.

When Mozambique achieved independence, the new Communist government tried to suppress family customs. It expected Mozambicans to shift their loyalties from their lineages and clans to cooperative farms and villages. This demand met strong resistance. Most farmers held onto their private plots, stayed in their own homes, and kept farming for their own families.

Most Mozambican families still practice subsistence farming. By long tradition, men plow the land with oxen or tractors. Women weed, water, and harvest the crops.

Until recently, Mozambican women have had limited social roles and few legal rights. They usually got little education, married young, and lived strictly domestic lives. They had no right to seek employment, make career decisions, or keep marital property after divorce. Women's roles in Mozambique are slowly changing. In 2003 the Assembly of the Republic passed the Family Law. It guarantees girls and women the rights to education, later marriage, equitable divorce, and authority over their own careers. In the south, many women have taken charge as their husbands and fathers have left the country to work in South African mines. Throughout Mozambique, many women hold important government positions. Some have joined the military. But girls still face educational obstacles. Many rural families don't send their daughters to school. Instead, the girls tend their families' farms and homes.

Religion

Mozambique's population includes a large community of Christians (people who follow the teachings of Jesus). This community is a legacy of colonial-era missionaries. About 50 percent of Mozambicans claim Christianity as their main faith. Within this group, Roman Catholics account for 24 percent. Christian Zionists make up another 18 percent, while other Protestant groups form about 8 percent.

Arab traders introduced Islam in the 700s. About 20 percent of Mozambicans are Muslims, or followers of Islam. Muslims believe that Allah (God) gave messages to Muhammad through the angel Gabriel. The holy scriptures of the Quran contain these messages. This religion is widespread in northern Mozambique. Mozambican Muslims, like

Catholics attend Mass in central Mozambique. The Portuguese brought Roman Catholicism to Mozambique in the 1500s.

Muslim men and boys take part in a prayer meeting in a town on the central coast of Mozambique. Arab traders brought Islam to Africa in the A.D. 700s.

Muslims in other countries, belong to different branches (such as Sunni and Shiite) and sects (such as Sufi). The Yao ethnic group of the north is almost entirely Muslim.

Ten percent of the population practices animism. Some Mozambican ethnic groups, such as the Makonde, have consistently resisted outside faiths and have held to their traditional animistic beliefs. In addition, many Mozambicans mix Christianity and Islam with animism. About 20 percent of Mozambicans belong to no organized religion.

Language

The official language of Mozambique is Portuguese. The government made this decision to avoid power struggles among the country's many ethnic groups. Each group speaks a different language or dialect (regional variation of a major language). Portuguese is a Romance language. Like Spanish and French, Portuguese developed from Latin, the ancient language of the Roman Empire. Fewer than 10 percent of Mozambicans speak Portuguese on a daily basis. However, it serves many citizens as a second language. Portuguese appears in government documents, on state-run television, in print media, and on Mozambique's official websites.

Bantu languages are the everyday languages of most Mozambicans. Macua and Lomue are widely spoken in the north. Tsonga is dominant in the south and in parts of eastern South Africa. The Chopi dialect is common around the port of Inhambane. A very common language along the coast—and throughout eastern Africa—is Swahili. About half of Mozambicans speak Swahili as a second language. Within Mozambique, Swahili and other Bantu languages incorporate Portuguese words and phrases.

Both Portuguese and Swahili serve Mozambique's small communities of Arabs and Indians, who also speak the languages of their ancestors. English usage is growing, particularly in business and higher education. The government requires public schools to teach some English.

◉ Literature

Mozambique has a long tradition of sung poetry and folktales. Portuguese explorers who first encountered the Tsonga found them using conch shells (large spiral seashells) and marimbas (xylophone-like instruments) to accompany their storytelling. Songs of praise and criticism served to inform, to express public opinion, and to entertain. Births, weddings, funerals, and other community events provided opportunities for storytellers to recount family histories and teach moral lessons. Oral literature still thrives among the Chopi and many other ethnic groups—especially those living outside the cities.

Many Mozambican writers see the poet Rui de Noronha as the founder of their country's modern literary tradition. He was born in 1909 and became a civil servant (government worker). Literary journals published his poems throughout his life. But he never realized his dream of publishing his works in a book. After his death in 1943, a group of friends collected and published his poems in the book *Sonetos*.

José Craveirinha (1922–2003) wrote poetry criticizing Portuguese rule of Mozambique. After he joined FRELIMO, the Portuguese arrested and imprisoned him. When Mozambique gained independence, Craveirinha became a government press official. He also became one of the country's leading poets, publishing his work in journals throughout Africa.

The violence and hardship of Mozambique's war for independence were important subjects for Marcelino dos Santos. He was born in 1929 and studied in Lisbon, the capital of Portugal. He fled Portugal when his anticolonial poetry and prose earned him threats from the government. He formed an independence movement while living in Paris, France, and then became a founding member of FRELIMO. He used his writing and speaking talent to promote Mozambican independence throughout the world. In 1970 he became the vice president of Mozambique.

Mia Couto (born in 1955) is one of the best-known writers in the Portuguese language. His vivid novels describe the stress of living with civil war and being uprooted. His first novel, *Sleepwalking Land*, earned praise. He followed it with many more books, including novels, short story collections, children's books, and nonfiction.

Eduardo White (born in 1963) has published eight books of poetry and helped found the literary journal *Charrua*. He has also won several important Mozambican literary awards. In his short poems—often about love—he experiments with form, style, and language.

▶ Art and Crafts

Mozambican craft artists work in many different media and styles. The Makonde people of northern Mozambique are well known for their wood carving. Makonde artists are best known for the wooden masks they use in ceremonies and dances. They also craft elongated sculptures in ebony (a black hardwood). These sculptures are called *shetani* (a Swahili word meaning "spirit"). *Ujamaa* are also tall ebony carvings. They resemble totem poles. Many ujamaa tell the story of a family and portray its important members.

Traditional masks carved from hardwood are for sale at a local market.

Mozambique's most renowned artist, Malangatana Ngwenya, has shown his paintings in galleries throughout Africa and the world since 1959. Many of his works are large public murals. Sculptor Alberto Chissano belonged to the same circle of Maputo artists as Ngwenya. Both expressed anti-Portuguese ideas in their works, and both became famous figures after independence.

Music and Dance

Portuguese music strongly influenced Mozambican performers and composers before the country gained independence. After 1975 its musicians turned to African folk and modern music.

The Makonde are known for the *lupembe*, wind instruments they create from animal horns, gourds, or wood. The *timbila*, another xylophone-like instrument, is popular among the Chopi people. Timbila orchestras contain up to ten performers. The players weave complex melodies in different tempos to accompany dancers. Eduardo Durão and Venancio Mbande have won fame as timbila musicians.

The *marrabenta* style developed in Maputo in the 1970s. It has since become one of the most popular musical styles in southern Africa. This lively dance music combines electric, wind, and percussion instruments. The Orchestra Marrabenta Star de Moçambique, led by the singer Wazimbo, has gained worldwide fame for its recordings and live concerts. This group has helped spread marrabenta music far beyond the borders of Mozambique.

South African artist Jimmy Dludlu (with guitar) plays with Mozambican musicians on traditional timbilas.

Women in a village of northern Mozambique perform a dance that involves jumping rope.

Mozambican villagers hold traditional dances for many different religious and social occasions. The *mapiko* is a dance that represents the return of the dead and the protection of the living from their terrors. Makonde men perform it while masked and costumed from head to toe. The *tufo* is a dance popular in northern Mozambique. It began as a Muslim dance in praise of Muhammad, but it has developed into other forms too. Women usually perform it. The Chopi of the south have developed several different dance forms, to accompany the *midogo*, played by a timbila orchestra.

Food

Mozambican cooks prepare meals around their staple foods: corn, rice, cassava (a starchy root), and the grain millet. Meals throughout the day often include corn porridge or fried potatoes. When meat is available, people add spices and stew, fry, or boil it and serve it with vegetables such as beans or squash. Fresh seafood—prawns, squid, lobster, and crabs—is plentiful along the coast.

The specialties of Mozambique reflect both African and Portuguese influences. People make thick *matata* stew with seafood (usually clams) cooked in wine and mixed with chopped peanuts and vegetables. They flavor a dish called *caril* with curry (a mixture of spices) and boiled fruit such as mango. Cooks have adopted garlic, tomatoes, and avocados from the cuisines of Portugal and Brazil. Tropical foods such as cashews, coconut, papaya, and pineapple are common ingredients combined with chicken, beef, or other meats. Mozambican cooks spice up many of their dishes with a hot pepper sauce called *piri piri*.

MATATA

This spicy clam-and-peanut stew is one of Mozambique's most popular dishes. Mozambican cooks usually add pumpkin leaves, but this recipe substitutes spinach. Those who don't like their food too spicy can skip the red pepper or use less.

1 cup chopped onions

4 to 5 tablespoons olive oil

2 6.5-ounce cans chopped clams, drained

1 cup chopped peanuts

2 tomatoes, diced

1 teaspoon salt

½ teaspoon black pepper

1 teaspoon crushed red pepper

1 bunch spinach leaves, thoroughly washed and finely chopped

1. Sauté the onions in olive oil in a large saucepan until soft.
2. Add the chopped clams, peanuts, diced tomatoes, salt, black pepper, and red pepper. Simmer on low heat for 30 minutes.
3. Add the spinach leaves and cover tightly. When the leaves have wilted (about 5 minutes later), serve matata over cooked rice.

Makes 4 to 6 servings.

A light breakfast offers *cha* (tea) or coffee, sweet breads, and sometimes fresh fish. The midday meal is usually the largest meal of the day. It often consists of sandwiches or rice dishes from street vendors. *Jantar* (dinner) is a smaller meal of a simple dish served with corn porridge or rice. For dessert, hosts serve fresh or sugared fruit, rice puddings, or sweet doughnuts. Coffee, tea, soft drinks, fruit juices, and bottled water are popular beverages. Adults also sample palm or grape wine or corn beer.

◗ Holidays

Several public holidays celebrate Mozambique's struggle for independence. February 3 is Heroes' Day, when Mozambicans honor their nation's founders. Independence Day, June 25, marks the date in 1975 when Mozambique won freedom from Portugal. September 7 is Lusaka Agreement Day, or Victory Day, which recalls the treaty that ended Mozambique's war with Portugal. Armed Forces Day on September 25 honors the day on which armed rebellion against Portugal began.

Other important public holidays are New Year's Day (January 1), Women's Day (April 7), Workers' Day (May 1), and Peace Day (October 4). On December 25, Christians celebrate Christmas, while non-Christians celebrate Family Day.

Sports and Recreation

During the war years, leisure activities vanished as Mozambicans either joined the fray or simply tried to stay alive. In the 1990s, the return of peace finally allowed Mozambicans to enjoy competitive sports and recreation.

The most popular organized sports in Mozambique are basketball, *futebol* (soccer), and cricket (a baseball-like game). Many Mozambicans play these sports informally or in community leagues. The Mozambican Basketball Federation, the Mozambican Soccer Federation, and the Mozambican Cricket Association organize play at the top levels.

Among individual sports, track and field has found a wide audience. Mozambican runner Maria Mutola is a world-class competitor in the 800-meter dash. At the 2000 Summer Olympics in Sydney, Australia, Mutola won the country's first Olympic gold medal.

Mozambique's national parks offer many opportunities for hiking and wildlife viewing. Sport fishing, scuba diving, and snorkeling are popular among tourists who visit the seacoast and the many small islands, where large coral reefs still flourish.

Mozambique's top basketball player is Clarisse Machanguana, a 6-foot 5-inch (2 m) center. With her help, Mozambique's national team won a gold medal in 2006 at the first-ever Lusophony Games held by the world's Portuguese-speaking countries. Machanguana has also played for three teams in the U.S. Women's National Basketball Association (WNBA).

In 2006 **Maria Mutola** won the women's 800-meter final at the International Association of Athletic Federations (IAAF) World Indoor Championships in Moscow. At the age of thirty-five, Mutola competed in the 800-meters in the 2008 Beijing Olympics and came in fifth.

THE ECONOMY

Mozambique's civil war dealt a heavy blow to the nation's economy. The war damaged roads and bridges, closed mines and factories, and uprooted many farmers and workers. The Communist system in place during those years also hurt the economy. Both productivity and foreign investment dropped. By the end of the war in 1992, Mozambique's economy had ground to a halt, and its people were among the poorest in the world.

Mozambique gradually recovered through the 1990s. Peace and stability attracted investment from Portugal and from southern African neighbors. As war refugees returned home, they provided a large supply of cheap labor. This in turn encouraged business growth.

The 1990s also brought an end to Communism in Mozambique. The government privatized (sold to private owners) more than one thousand state-owned businesses. With the government no longer controlling business activities, companies had to compete with one another in a free market. To ensure profit and survival, many had to

lay off workers and begin charging higher prices for their goods and services. In the early twenty-first century, most Mozambican businesses are private. But the government still owns important public services, such as ports, railroads, utilities, and telecommunications companies.

Mozambique's fast-rising gross domestic product (GDP) reflects its economic recovery. (The GDP is the total value of goods and services produced inside the country in one year.) In 2006 Mozambique's GDP reached about $17 billion, or about $800 per person. The GDP is growing at the rate of about 8 percent every year. This makes Mozambique one of the fastest-growing economies in Africa.

⊙ Services

Mozambique's service sector includes banking, transportation, wholesale and retail trade, business services, telecommunications, hotels, bars, restaurants, tourism, housing, and government services. The sector accounts for about 53 percent of the nation's GDP. This GDP share has grown steadily since 1992. It keeps growing as businesses damaged in the civil war rebuild and recover.

Service jobs employ about 13 percent of the nation's labor force. Many service workers take part in informal businesses that provide goods and services in steady demand, such as car maintenance, home repairs, and selling food and household goods in street markets. More and more people join this workforce as the government cuts spending and sells state-owned companies, both of which result in worker layoffs.

Mozambique is trying hard to develop its service sector. Services need few raw materials, tend to provide well-paid and steady employment, and bring in valuable foreign money. Like many other African nations, Mozambique is attracting a lot of foreign investment in service businesses—especially transportation and tourism.

Tourism in Mozambique is growing ever more important. Before the civil war, most visitors came from South Africa and Zimbabwe. In the twenty-first century, Mozambique attracts curious travelers from all over the world. The most important draw is the scenic coast of Inhambane Province in southern Mozambique. Other key attractions are historical sites on Mozambique Island, scuba diving and sport fishing in the Bazaruto Archipelago, and cultural activities in Maputo. Mozambique also promotes several large national parks. Among the

Visitors can relax poolside at the **Hotel Polana** in Maputo. Mozambique is working to develop its tourist industry.

most popular are Gorongosa National Park in central Mozambique and Great Limpopo Transfrontier Park in the south.

⊙ Industry

Mozambique's industrial sector includes manufacturing, mining, and energy. This sector is responsible for 27 percent of the nation's GDP. It employs 7 percent of the labor force.

While Mozambique was a colony, it served mainly as a source of raw materials for Portugal. Farming dominated the colonial economy. Industry went undeveloped because Portugal discouraged competition with its companies in Europe. In the 1970s, independence brought the birth of Mozambican industry. The major businesses were linked to agriculture. They processed and packaged rice, tea, sugar, and other cash crops for export.

Mozambique's industrial sector remains focused on foods, as well as on consumer goods such as clothing and furniture. Other factories refine chemicals into fertilizer and paint, crude oil into gasoline and other fuels, and bauxite into aluminum. Mozambique also has cement and glass factories.

The mining industry in Mozambique produces bauxite, gold, and graphite (a soft form of carbon). Gemstones are present in some river deposits, but gem mining is a small-scale business. Several companies are exploring for deposits of mineral sands along the coast. These deposits may produce useful ores such as titanium.

Aluminum produced in Mozambique is baled and ready for export.

Mozambique has a variety of energy resources. It doesn't currently produce oil, but geologists are exploring for oil deposits offshore. Mozambique does have sizable natural gas and coal deposits. Natural gas is an important export. However, the country needs more foreign investment to develop its large coal reserves. The Cahora Bassa Dam generates enough electricity for Mozambican use and for sale to neighboring countries.

Agriculture

Mozambique's agricultural sector includes farming, fishing, and forestry. This sector is responsible for 20 percent of the nation's GDP. It employs about 80 percent of Mozambican workers.

Most of these people live and work on small farms. The farms produce staple foods such as corn, rice, and cassava as well as cash crops such as cotton, cashews, coconuts, tropical fruits, rice, tea, and sisal (a plant used to make rope). The main livestock are beef and dairy cattle, poultry, pigs, and goats. The most productive farming regions are the Zambezi River valley and the southern coast. These areas get plenty of rain and have fertile soil. Other regions are drier, and outside the river valleys the soil is poor.

Privatization has been good for Mozambican agriculture. But the country has room for further rural development. Only about 12 percent of the farmable land is cultivated. Poor roads and limited transportation services prevent many farmers from getting their harvest to public markets. The cost of seed, fertilizer, and tools poses an obstacle too. Many farmers have banded together into rural cooperatives that allow them easier access to these necessary items.

Floodwaters from the Zambezi River surround a town in Tete Province.
Floods are an annual threat to the lives and economy of Mozambique.

The floods of the early twenty-first century dealt a major blow to agriculture. Most Mozambican farms lie on floodplains near the major rivers. One bad flood can ruin a whole year's harvest and destroy livestock herds. After flooding, the country must import food (buy food from other nations) to feed the people displaced from their farms and villages. Farmers must also rebuild their property and recover their losses. Mozambique still does not produce enough food for all its citizens.

Along the seacoast and rivers, fishing is an important agricultural activity. Commercial fishing boats on the Indian Ocean haul in tuna, herring, anchovies, mackerel, and prawns. Prawns are the country's biggest export. The Mozambican fishing fleet has overfished coastal waters, however, and the shellfish populations there are shrinking. Mozambique's inland waters produce tilapia (a food fish) as well as Nile crocodiles for their skins, which are used in high-fashion items such as shoes and purses.

Forestry is another important part of Mozambique's agricultural sector. Fuelwood supplies about 80 percent of the energy Mozambicans use. (Natural gas, coal, hydropower, and imported oil supply the other 20 percent.) The country's forests also produce both hardwood and soft-wood timber. The government supports and promotes eucalyptus tree plantations. These plantations provide cheap softwood for Mozambican use and save valuable hardwood for export. Other important forest products are wood pulp, grass, bamboo, reed, medicinal plants, and wild edible plants.

Transportation and Communications

Mozambique has spent a lot of money repairing its transportation system—especially roads and rails—after decades of war. Nevertheless, the country still lacks good roads. Reliable shipping and train service is still unavailable in many areas.

The road network extends about 18,890 miles (30,401 km). But only 3,533 miles (5,686 km) are paved. Long distances and poor roads separate smaller inland towns from larger coastal cities. Travel between major cities requires long, slow journeys too. Private bus companies offer reliable daily service. Many Mozambicans travel by *chapas*, which are trucks with benches for passengers.

Mozambique's rail system consists of 1,945 miles (3,130 km) of track. This system is very important to Mozambique's neighbors. For the landlocked nations of Malawi, Zambia, Zimbabwe, and Swaziland, Mozambican railways provide key links to international shipping routes. Railroads join these neighbors—as well as South African mines—with the ports of Nacala, Beira, and Maputo.

The port of Maputo offers oceangoing ships a deepwater harbor. Maputo is the busiest port on Africa's southeastern coast. Mozambique's neighbors export many of their goods and raw materials through this

In 1910 French architect Gustave Eiffel designed the **Maputo railway station.** Eiffel was famous for his 1889 Eiffel Tower in Paris, France.

Ships dock at the Maputo harbor. Roads and rail lines connect Maputo with Johannesburg, South Africa, and other inland cities.

port. Beira and Nacala also have docking and loading facilities for cargo ships. Inhambane is a busy leisure port, with many cruises and day trips available for tourists. Many ferries sail between the coastal cities and major offshore islands.

Mozambique has twenty-two airports with paved runways. The largest are the international airports at Maputo and Beira. Mozambique Airlines (better known by its Portuguese acronym, LAM) flies between major cities and to foreign destinations.

Mozambique's telecommunications system suffered heavy damage during the civil war. As a result, the nation's system of fixed telephone lines is still very limited. Most Mozambicans use mobile phones and have no landlines installed in their homes. About thirty radio stations, as well as one state-controlled TV station, broadcast in Mozambique. Some urban families have access to satellite television.

Foreign Trade

Mozambique buys more goods, services, and raw materials from foreign countries than it sells to them. The main Mozambican imports are heavy machinery, transportation equipment, electronic goods, food, and fuels. Mozambique's key import partners are its southern African neighbors—especially Zimbabwe and South Africa.

These women work at a **cashew processing plant** in Maputo. Mozambique was the world's largest cashew provider in the 1970s, but civil war disrupted cashew production. The government, international agencies, and farmers are working to find ways for Mozambique to regain its lead in cashew production, a labor-intensive industry.

These nations are also key to Mozambique's developing export business. They buy electricity generated by Mozambique's hydropower projects. These projects are a valuable and growing source of income for Mozambique. Other important industrial exports are titanium, tantalum, and aluminum. The fishing fleet sends prawns and other shellfish to markets in Asia and Europe. Mozambican farms export cotton, sugar, tea, fruits, cashews, and copra (dried coconut).

To produce copra, Mozambicans dry coconut flesh in the sun. Processors then remove the flesh from the shell. They press the flesh to extract coconut oil. This useful product goes into margarine, soap, and suntan lotion.

Mozambique is trying to expand its export business, which earns valuable foreign currency. Export businesses also attract foreign investment, which spurs further development. Mozambique has already attracted investment from Europe, China, and South Africa.

The Future

Although Mozambique has worked hard to recover from its civil war, it's still wrestling with rural reconstruction. The war displaced many families, and their farms lie in need of repair. Some roads and bridges are still impassable. Public schools and basic services are in short supply. And many regions still lack enough food, basic housing, and medicine. Drought and flooding have aggravated these rural problems.

Mozambique has been **building hotels,** such as this one, to boost its tourism industry.

However, Mozambique's rebuilding efforts are beginning to pay off. The end of Communism in Mozambique in the 1990s began a period of rapid economic growth. Rapid growth often leads to inflation (rising prices), but the Mozambican government has managed to keep prices under control. And recently, it has been able to funnel some resources to new development.

Among Mozambique's various economic development efforts, tourism and hydroelectricity promise to be important sources of income. The stable Mozambican government is also good for business. Although bitter political disputes occasionally erupt, the factions have learned to coexist peacefully.

The country's rebuilding efforts and welcoming business climate have drawn investment from several foreign nations. Some have forgiven Mozambique's debt, which speeds economic recovery. Others are pouring money into industries and transportation services. Thanks to prolonged peace and hard work, Mozambique finally has a chance to prosper.

For links to more information about Mozambique's economy, visit www.vgsbooks.com.

Timeline

CA. 10,000 B.C. Nomadic hunters inhabit southeastern Africa.

A.D. 300 Bantu-speaking peoples expanding through southern Africa reach the Zambezi River valley and the Indian Ocean.

700s Arab merchants set up trading ports on Africa's southeastern coast.

1100 A slave trade begins between Arabia and the ports of southeastern Africa.

1200 The Munhumutapa Empire arises in southern Africa.

1498 Explorer Vasco da Gama rounds the Cape of Good Hope and lands on Mozambique Island, claiming it for Portugal.

1502 The Portuguese overthrow the Arab sultanate at Sofala.

1505 Portuguese explorer Franciso de Almeida reaches Sofala and Mozambique Island.

1507 Portugal establishes a capital on Mozambique Island to govern its colony of Portuguese East Africa.

1561 Portugal begins taking command of southeast African gold-trading routes.

1580 Spain and Portugal unite. The king ignores Portuguese colonies in Africa, and trade declines there.

1605 Dutch raiding parties try—but ultimately fail—to take over Portuguese ports on the Indian Ocean.

1629 Portugal seizes the Munhumutapa Empire and begins leasing prazos.

1640 The union of Spain and Portugal ends.

1777 Austrian ships raid the port of Lourenço Marques.

1790s-1820s Mozambique's slave trade booms.

1842 Portugal outlaws the slave trade, driving it underground, where it continues to thrive.

1884-1885 The Berlin Conference confirms Portugal's right in European eyes to govern Portuguese East Africa.

1898 Lourenço Marques becomes the capital of Portuguese East Africa.

1914-1918 World War I takes place. Portugal joins the Allies and drafts African men to fight, sparking violent resistance.

1926   The dictatorship of António Salazar begins in Portugal.

1939-1945   World War II takes place. Portugal and its colonies stay neutral.

1951   Portugal renames Portuguese East Africa Mozambique and declares it a province of Portugal.

1962   Led by Eduardo Mondlane, Mozambicans found FRELIMO in Tanzania.

1964   FRELIMO begins an armed uprising against Portuguese control of Mozambique.

1969   A letter bomb kills Mondlane.

1970   Samora Machel takes over leadership of FRELIMO.

1975   Mozambique officially gains independence and renames its capital Maputo. The Portuguese abruptly leave the country, forcing Mozambicans to rebuild their entire society.

1976   The RENAMO group is founded and begins sabotaging the FRELIMO government by raiding cities and farms, killing and terrorizing civilians, and destroying infrastructure. The civil war begins.

1986   President Samora Machel dies in a plane crash.

1990   The FRELIMO government passes a new constitution ending many of its Communist policies.

1992   FRELIMO and RENAMO sign a peace treaty in Rome, Italy, ending the civil war.

1994   Mozambique holds its first democratic elections. Joaquim Chissano becomes president.

1999   Chissano wins a second presidential term.

2000   Maria Mutola wins Mozambique's first Olympic gold medal. Floods devastate coastal areas and river valleys.

2004   Armando Guebuza wins the presidential election.

2008   Cyclone Jokwe strikes the coast of Mozambique, causing heavy rains and flooding.

COUNTRY NAME Republic of Mozambique

AREA 302,739 square miles (784,090 sq. km)

MAIN LANDFORMS Coastal plains, Mavia Plateau, Namuli Highlands, Angonia Highlands, Tete Highlands, Zambezi River valley, Manica Plateau, Chimanimani Mountains, Gorongosa Mountains, Lebombo Mountains, southern plains

HIGHEST POINT Mount Binga, 7,992 feet (2,436 m) above sea level

LOWEST POINT Sea level

MAJOR RIVERS Zambezi, Limpopo, Pungwe, Rovuma

ANIMALS antelopes, Cape buffalo, cheetahs, cobras, dolphins, dugongs, elephants, giraffes, hippopotamuses, leopards, lions, Nile crocodiles, puff adders, pythons, sharks, whales, wildebeests, zebras

CAPITAL CITY Maputo

OTHER MAJOR CITIES Beira, Nampula, Quelimane

OFFICIAL LANGUAGE Portuguese

MONETARY UNIT Metical. 100 centavos = 1 metical.

CURRENCY

Mozambique's currency is the metical. Its international currency code is MZN, and its written symbol is MTn. The government introduced the metical in 1980 to replace the escudo, the Portuguese currency in circulation at the time. Coins come in denominations of 1, 5, 10, 20, and 50 centavos and 1, 2, 5, and 10 meticals. Paper notes come in denominations of 20, 50, 100, 200, 500, and 1,000 meticals.

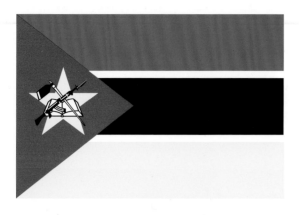

Mozambique adopted its current flag on May 1, 1983. The flag displays, three wide horizontal bands of green, black, and yellow separated by thin white bands. On the hoist side, a red triangle contains a yellow star, a white open book, and a black hoe and rifle. Green stands for Mozambique's fertile land. Yellow stands for the country's minerals, black for the continent of Africa, and white for justice and peace. Red represents the struggle for independence. The star is a Communist symbol borrowed from the Soviet Union. The book symbolizes education, the hoe stands for farming, and the rifle represents Mozambicans' determination to protect their freedom.

The first national anthem of independent Mozambique was "Viva, Viva a FRELIMO" (Long Live FRELIMO). In 2002 the government adopted a new anthem, "Pátria Amada" (Beloved Homeland). Both anthems are the work of Justino Chemane.

Beloved Homeland
In the memory of Africa and the world
Beautiful homeland of those who dared to fight
Mozambique, your name is freedom
And your June sun will forever shine.
People united from Ruvuma to Maputo
Harvest the fruits of the fight for peace
The dream grows waving in the flag
And is planted in the certainty of tomorrow.

Flowers sprouting in the soil of your sweat
For mountains, for the rivers, for the sea
We swear by you, O Mozambique
No tyrant will enslave us.

Mozambique, our glorious land
Stone by stone constructing a new day
Millions of arms, only one force
O beloved homeland, we will prevail.

 Visit www.vgsbooks.com for links to listen to Mozambique's national anthem.

Flag   National Anthem

FRANCISCO DE ALMEIDA (1450–1510) Almeida was a Portuguese soldier and explorer born in Lisbon, Portugal. The king of Portugal, Manuel I, appointed Almeida viceroy (colonial governor) of India in 1503. Two years later, Almeida set out with a large fleet, rounded the Cape of Good Hope, and reached the coast of East Africa. The fleet anchored at Sofala and Mozambique Island, strengthening Portugal's claims on the region.

PAULINA CHIZIANE (b. 1955) Chiziane is a novelist born in Manjacaze in southern Mozambique. She attended Eduardo Mondlane University in Maputo. With *Balada do Amor ao Vento*, she became the first published female novelist in Mozambique's history. She has written several other novels and short story collections, including *Ventos do Apocalipse* and *O Sétimo Juramento*.

JOSÉ CRAVEIRINHA (1922–2003) Craveirinha is the most famous Mozambican poet. He was born in Lourenço Marques. He began his career writing articles and poems—many critical of Portugal—for Portuguese literary magazines. After he joined FRELIMO, the Portuguese arrested and imprisoned him for four years. After Mozambique gained independence, the government made him a press minister.

AFONSO DHLAKAMA (b. 1953) Dhlakama is a political leader born in Mangunde. He succeeded André Matsangaissa as the leader of RENAMO during the early 1980s. Dhlakama oversaw RENAMO's transformation from a guerrilla army into a political organization. He ran for president of Mozambique in 1994, 1999, and 2004. Although he lost all three elections, within RENAMO he remains a popular figure.

SAMORA MACHEL (1933–1986) Machel was a FRELIMO leader and the first president of independent Mozambique. Born in Madragoa (modern Chilembene) into a Shangan family, he studied nursing in Lourenço Marques. He joined FRELIMO in 1962 and led its first assault against the Portuguese in 1964. He became president in 1975. Under his leadership, the country struggled to rebuild its society while fighting the opposition group RENAMO. He died in a plane crash in 1986.

GRAÇA MACHEL-MANDELA (b. 1945) Born in the village of Incadine, Machel-Mandela is the widow of Samora Machel. She later married Nelson Mandela, a former president of South Africa. She attended the University of Lisbon and afterward joined FRELIMO. She was active in the fight for independence. The FRELIMO-led government named her minister for education and culture. She has long been working to benefit Mozambican refugee children.

EDUARDO MONDLANE (1920–1969) Mondlane was a founder and first president of FRELIMO. Born in Gaza Province in southern Mozambique, he was the son of a Tsonga chieftain. He studied at the University of Lisbon, Oberlin College in Ohio, and Northwestern University in Illinois. He helped found FRELIMO in 1962 and called for an independent, Communist Mozambique. He led FRELIMO in its war against the Portuguese until a letter bomb killed him in 1969.

GABRIEL ESTÊVÃO MONJANE (1944–1990) Monjane was one of the few people in recorded history to grow taller than 8 feet (2.4 m). He was the tallest African ever at an official height of 8 feet 1 inch (2.5 m). Born in Manjacaze, he joined a circus at the age of seventeen. He was the tallest living person in the world during the late 1980s. He suffered chronic health problems due to his size. He died after falling in his home.

MARIA MUTOLA (b. 1972) Mutola is a runner from Maputo. She specializes in the 800-meter dash. She began her athletic career as a talented soccer player who won the attention and support of the poet José Craveirinha. She competed in the 1988 Summer Olympics at the age of fifteen. She dominated the 800-meter event through the 1990s, winning several gold medals in international competitions. She won a bronze medal at the 1996 Summer Olympics in Atlanta, Georgia, and a gold medal at the 2000 Summer Olympics in Sydney, Australia.

MALANGATANA NGWENYA (b. 1936) Ngwenya is a Mozambican painter and poet. He often exhibits work under his first name. Born in the village of Matalana, he moved to Lourenço Marques as a teenager and began showing his art professionally in 1959. The Portuguese jailed him in 1964 for his opposition to the colonial government. After his release, he won renown as a painter and muralist, winning many commissions to decorate public buildings and spaces.

GONCALO DA SILVEIRA (1526–1561) Silveira was a Catholic priest and missionary born in Almeirim, Portugal. Silveira was appointed to an important colonial post in India in 1555. After three years, he left to do missionary work in southern Africa. He landed at Sofala and journeyed inland along the Zambezi River. He baptized a ruler of the Munhumutapa Empire, as well as several thousand subjects, but was murdered after Arab traders spread rumors of his intentions.

SOSHANGANE (?–1856) Soshangane was a Zulu leader who founded a realm called Gaza in southern Mozambique. He rebelled against Shaka, the supreme ruler of the Zulus, and fled into Mozambique with a large group of followers. This force defeated the Portuguese in the coastal settlements and around Delagoa Bay (modern Maputo Bay) and made them pay tribute to his realm. After his death, Gaza declined until its defeat by Europeans in 1895.

BAZARUTO ARCHIPELAGO This group of islands off the coast of Inhambane Province became the Bazaruto Archipelago National Marine Park in 1971. Visitors can tour the islands in dhows (traditional eastern African sailboats) and watch dolphins, dugongs, and other wildlife. The islands also offer diving, snorkeling, and pristine white-sand beaches.

GORONGOSA NATIONAL PARK This large park in central Mozambique includes Mount Gorongosa, a sacred place to many area residents. The park offers visitors a look at an amazing variety of terrain and living species. Its plants and animals are finally recovering from the deforestation and poaching they suffered during the civil war.

IRON HOUSE This building in downtown Maputo is made entirely of steel. Gustave Eiffel, architect of the famous Eiffel Tower in Paris, France, designed the Iron House in 1892. It was meant as a residence for the governor of Portuguese East Africa, but in the time before air-conditioning, it proved much too hot for comfort. Various government ministries have used it for offices instead.

LAKE MALAWI This large lake separates Malawi and northwestern Mozambique. Its clear waters teem with hundreds of fish species, and very little human development clutters its shores. Few roads to the lakeshore exist in Mozambique. Most visitors arrange a guided 4x4 (all-terrain vehicle) expedition to reach it.

MAPUTO SPECIAL RESERVE This small tract of protected land lies in southern Mozambique, not far from Maputo. It's home to a thriving herd of wild elephants, as well as hippos, antelope, gazelles, crocodiles, and other wildlife.

MOZAMBIQUE ISLAND This island is the site of Vasco da Gama's landing in 1498. It was also the first Portuguese capital of Mozambique. The island is home to San Sebastian of Mozambique, a sixteenth-century fortress. It is the oldest European fort in sub-Saharan Africa (south of the Sahara).

animism: a system of belief in spirits that inhabit natural places, beings, things, and the everyday world and that influence human lives and fortunes

assimilado: in Mozambique an African who has adopted the language and culture of the Portuguese

Bantu: an African language group that many eastern African ethnic groups use

capitalism: an economic system characterized by private ownership of property and by prices determined in free markets

cassava: a root plant that is a staple of the Mozambican diet

colony: a territory controlled by a foreign power

Communism: a political and economic theory supporting community ownership of all property. Its goal is to create equality.

constitution: a document defining the basic principles and laws of a nation

deforestation: the loss of forests due to logging or clearing land for human uses. Deforestation leads to soil erosion and loss of wildlife habitat.

democratic: governed by representatives freely elected by the people

FRELIMO: a group founded in 1962 that opposed Portuguese rule of Mozambique. FRELIMO is the dominant political party in independent Mozambique.

hydroelectric power: electricity produced by damming a river and then harnessing the energy of rushing water at hydroelectric power stations

indigena: in Mozambique an African who has kept his or her traditional language and culture

Munhumutapa: an empire established by Shona rulers that arose in southern Africa (modern Zimbabwe) in the 1200s. It ruled much of Mozambique through the 1500s.

prazeiros: landlords who leased large land estates in Mozambique while it was a colony of Portugal. Most prazeiros used their land for farming or mining and forced African residents to be their labor force.

prazo: a vast land estate leased by Mozambique's colonial government to attract farmers and settlers to the interior

RENAMO: a rebel group founded in Zimbabwe and supported by Zimbabwe and South Africa, which fought to unseat the FRELIMO government after Mozambique's independence in 1975

Shona: a large ethnic group of southern Africa, with members living in Zimbabwe, South Africa, and Mozambique

Swahili: a language that developed along the east African coast. It combines words from Arabic and Bantu languages.

Zulu: a large warrior society that conquered and occupied large stretches of southern Africa in the 1700s and early 1800s

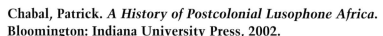

Selected Bibliography

Chabal, Patrick. *A History of Postcolonial Lusophone Africa.* **Bloomington: Indiana University Press, 2002.**
The author describes the troubled histories of five Portuguese African colonies, including Mozambique, after they won independence.

Elkiss, T. H. *The Quest for an African El Dorado: Sofala, Southern Zambezia, and the Portuguese, 1500–1865.* **Waltham, MA: Crossroads Press, 1981.**
This book offers a history of Portugal's failed drive to make Portuguese East Africa a profitable colony.

Englund, Harri. *From War to Peace on the Mozambique-Malawi Borderland.* **Edinburgh, UK: Edinburgh University Press, 2002.**
The author interviews villagers living along the Malawi-Mozambique border to understand the effects of civil war and its aftermath on the people living there.

FAO Country Profiles and Mapping Information System: Mozambique. 2008.
http://www.fao.org/countryprofiles/index.asp?lang=en&ISO3=MOZ (June 3, 2008).
This website links readers to detailed articles and maps describing the environment, economy, agriculture, forestry, and fishing of Mozambique.

Finnegan, William. *A Complicated War: The Harrowing of Mozambique.* **Berkeley: University of California Press, 1992.**
The author explores Mozambique in 1988 to discover the effects of its civil war on the people and economy. The book includes extensive historical background to explain the causes of the war.

Hanlon, Joseph. *Mozambique: The Revolution under Fire.* **London: Zed Books, 1990.**
The author discusses the interplay of international politics, economics, and foreign aid in Mozambique during the civil war years.

Hume, Cameron. *Ending Mozambique's War: The Role of Mediation and Good Offices.* **Washington, DC: United States Institute of Peace, 1994.**
A participant in the Rome peace talks, the author describes how mediators helped end Mozambique's civil war in 1992.

Mario, Azevedo, Emmanuel Nnadozie, and Tome Mbuia Joao. *Historical Dictionary of Mozambique.* **Lanham, MD: Scarecrow Press, 2004.**
This reference book offers helpful explanations of important events, people, places, and issues in the history of Mozambique.

Mondlane, Eduardo. *The Struggle for Mozambique.* **London: Penguin, 1969.**
In this book written during Mozambique's war for independence, the FRELIMO leader explains his outlook on Mozambique's colonial history and the means by which he intends to win self-rule for his country.

Newitt, Malyn. *A History of Mozambique.* **Bloomington: Indiana University Press, 1995.**
This long, detailed scholarly history of Mozambique includes a deep analysis of the civil war and its aftermath.

Pitcher, M. Anne. *Transforming Mozambique: The Politics of Privatization, 1975–2000.* **Cambridge: Cambridge University Press, 2000.**
The author discusses how Mozambique's government made the transformation from Communism to capitalism.

Population Reference Bureau. **May 23, 2008.**
http://www.prb.org (June 3, 2008).
The bureau offers current population figures, vital statistics, land area, and more. Special articles cover the latest environmental and health issues that concern each country.

Sanceau, Elaine. *The Land of Prester John: A Chronicle of Portuguese Exploration.* **Brighton, UK: Gardiner Press, 2007.**
This book provides a history of the many expeditions mounted by Portugal in the fifteenth and sixteenth centuries to explore and exploit the coasts of Africa, South America, and Asia.

Schafer, Jessica. *Soldiers at Peace: Veterans and Society after the Civil War in Mozambique.* **New York: Palgrave Macmillan, 2007.**
A scholarly study of soldiers who were demobilized after the civil war in Mozambique ended. The book examines the new peacetime roles the soldiers took up and the long-lasting effect of the conflict on their outlook and everyday life.

The World Factbook. **May 15, 2008.**
https://www.cia.gov/library/publications/the-world-factbook/geos/mz.html (June 3, 2008).
This website features up-to-date information about the people, land, economy, and government of Mozambique. It also briefly covers transnational issues.

BBC News Country Profile: Mozambique
http://news.bbc.co.uk/1/hi/world/africa/country_profiles/1063120.stm
This helpful site provides a quick overview of Mozambique's recent history, political events, and economic development.

Couto, Mia, and David Brookshaw. *Sleepwalking Land*. London: Serpent's Tail, 2006.
This novel describes the adventure of two refugees, an old man and a young boy, who seek safety together during the civil war.

Fitzpatrick, Mary. *Mozambique*. Oakland: Lonely Planet Publications, 2007.
This travel guide provides in-depth information on Mozambique's wide array of natural and historical landmarks, as well as on contemporary Mozambican culture. The book also includes a summary of the country's history and politics. Advice for travelers reveals many of the problems still affecting the daily life of Mozambique's citizens.

Hill, Pascoe G. *Fifty Days on. Board a Slave Vessel*. Baltimore: Black Classic Press, 1993.
In this book, a slave ship's doctor describes conditions during several weeks in the Mozambique Channel in 1843. Hill wrote this work, which includes many horrifying details, to help ban the slave trade.

King, David C. *Cultures of the World: Mozambique*. New York: Benchmark Books, 2007.
In this book for young adults, the author reviews Mozambique's history and culture, giving a wealth of details on the various ethnic groups living within the country and their art, writing, food, recreation, holidays, and traditions.

Languages of Mozambique
http://www.ethnologue.com/show_country.asp?name=Mozambique
This website provides detailed descriptions of the many languages and dialects spoken in Mozambique, including locations, alternate names, and classifications.

Lonely Planet Mozambique: Overview
http://www.lonelyplanet.com/worldguide/mozambique
This handy online traveler's guide gives up-to-date information on conditions within Mozambique, summarizes the nation's culture and background, and guides travelers to notable parks, historic sites, beaches, islands, and cities.

Mozambique: Latest News and Features
http://www.irinnews.org/Africa-Country.aspx?Country=MZ
This United Nations site offers frequently updated news and articles on humanitarian efforts in Mozambique.

Mozambique News Agency
http://www.poptel.org.uk/mozambique-news/
This site offers readers a directory of biweekly reports—in Portuguese and English—on current events in Mozambique.

Ndege, George O. *Culture and Customs of Mozambique.* **Westport, CT: Greenwood Press, 2006.**

The author of this book describes family life and culture in modern Mozambique, discussing ethnic groups, religion, customs, literature, fine arts, and other topics important to understanding the country and its people.

Sheldon, Kathleen E. *Pounders of Grain: A History of Women, Work, and Politics in Mozambique.* **Portsmouth, NH: Heinemann, 2002.**

In this book, the author gives a history of Mozambican women and their experiences from the nineteenth to the twenty-first century. The book discusses traditional family structures, gender roles, the differences between patrilineal and matrilineal societies, and the transition from rural to urban life that many returning civil war refugees are making.

Stark, Peter. *At the Mercy of the River: An Exploration of the Last African Wilderness.* **New York: Ballantine Books, 2005.**

The author kayaks down the Lugenda River of northern Mozambique, encountering the many dangers of one of Earth's last true wilderness regions.

University of Pennsylvania African Studies Center: Mozambique Page
http://www.africa.upenn.edu/Country_Specific/Mozambique.html

This online directory provides links to many websites discussing Mozambican issues, including history, culture, government, geography, economy, and more.

Vermeulen, Jean-Paul. *Gone Diving Mozambique.* **Parker, CO: Outskirts Press, 2006.**

This book offers a photo essay and description of undersea adventures off the coast of Mozambique.

vgsbooks.com
http://www.vgsbooks.com

Visit vgsbooks.com, the home page of the Visual Geography Series®. You can get linked to all sorts of useful online information, including geographical, historical, demographic, cultural, and economic websites. The vgsbooks.com site is a great resource for late-breaking news and statistics.

West, Harry G. *Kupilikula: Governance and the Invisible Realm in Mozambique.* **Chicago: University of Chicago Press, 2005.**

This book explains the work of traditional medicine men and healers in northern Mozambican villages and how they interact with the country's modern politics.

Captions for photos appearing on cover and chapter openers:

Cover: Fishers on a traditional boat net a catch from off the northern coast of Mozambique.

pp. 4–5 Waves from the Indian Ocean crash on the white-sand shores of Mozambique. The country's eastern coastline stretches for 1,535 miles (2,470 km).

pp. 8–9 These inselbergs, or island mountains, are located in the Niassa Reserve in northern Mozambique. Inselbergs rise from the surrounding savanna like islands from the sea.

pp. 38–39 These children from southern Mozambique take a break from classes outside their one-room schoolhouse.

pp. 46–47 Women dance a traditional tufo dance that includes singing and dancing to the rhythms of drums and tambourines.

pp. 56–57 The Mercado Central is a large farmers' market in Maputo. Many farmers make a living by selling their fresh produce at local markets.

Photo Acknowledgments

The images in this book are used with the permission of: © P Groenendijk/Robert Harding/drr.net, pp. 4–5; © XNR Productions, pp. 6, 10; © Michael Fay/National Geographic/Getty Images, pp. 8–9; AP Photo/Themba Hadebe, pp. 11, 65; © Ariadne Van Zandbergen/Lonely Planet Images/Getty Images, p. 12; © Trygve Bolstad/ Panos Pictures, p. 13; © Paul Sutherland/National Geographic/Getty Images, p. 14; © Robbert Koene/Gallo Images ROOTS RF collection/Getty Images, p. 15; © Martin Harvey/The Image Bank/Getty Images, p. 17; © The Hebrew University of Jerusalem & The Jewish National & University Library, p. 22; © SuperStock, Inc./ SuperStock, p. 23; © Pedro Barretto de Resende/The Bridgeman Art Library/Getty Images, p. 25; © Mary Evans Picture Library/The Image Works, p. 26; The Granger Collection, New York, p. 29; © Popperfoto/Getty Images, p. 30; © Keystone/Hulton Archive/Getty Images, p. 31; AP Photo/dar/str, p. 32; © Peter Turnley/CORBIS, p. 34; © Kazuhiro NOGI/AFP/Getty Images, p. 35 (top); © Anders Gunnartz/Peter Arnold, Inc., p. 35 (bottom); AP Photo/Jockel Finck, p. 36; © David Larsen/africanpictures. net/The Image Works, pp. 38–39; © Ronald de Hommel/drr.net, p. 40; © Images of Africa Photobank/Alamy, p. 41 (top); © Volkmar K. Wentzel/National Geographic/ Getty Images, p. 41 (bottom); © Paco Campos/EFE/ZUMA Press, p. 43; © Jorgen Schytte/Peter Arnold, Inc., p. 44; © Liba Taylor/Robert Harding/drr.net, p. 45; © F.Rigaud/Travel-Images.com, pp. 46–47; © Dino Fracchia/drr.net, pp. 48, 49; © Oliver Strewe/Lonely Planet Images, p. 51; © Alfredo D'Amato/Panos Pictures, p. 52; © Bert de Ruiter/Alamy, p. 53; © Yuri Kadobnov/AFP/Getty Images, p. 55; © Ariadne Van Zandbergen/africanpictures.net /The Image Works, pp. 56–57; © imagebroker/Alamy, p. 58; © Graeme Williams/africanpictures.net/The Image Works, p. 59; © Friedrich Stark/Peter Arnold, Inc., p. 60; REUTERS/Grant Lee Neuenburg, p. 61; © G.Frysinger/Travel-Images.com, p. 62; © Jason Laure/Danita Delimont Agency/drr.net, p. 63; © ullstein-phalanx Fotoagentur/Peter Arnold, Inc., p. 64; Audrius Tomonis—www.banknotes.com, p. 68; © Laura Westlund/ Independent Picture Service, p. 69. Front cover: © Mike D. Kock/Gallo Images/ Getty Images. Back cover: NASA.